John Hollander, one of today's best known younger poets, studied at Columbia University, and received his Ph.D. from Indiana University. He has taught at the Connecticut College for Women, Yale University, and Hunter College, and has lectured widely in the United States and abroad. He is spending the 1967–1968 academic year in Cambridge, England, as Overseas Fellow at Churchill College.

Mr. Hollander was the recipient of the Yale Younger Poets Award in 1958, the Poetry Chap-Book Award in 1962, and a grant in Creative Writing from the American Institute of Arts and Letters in 1963. His publications include *A Crackling of Thorns* (1958), *The Untuning of the Sky: Ideas of Music in English Poetry, 1500–1700* (1961), *Movie-Going and Other Poems* (1962), *Visions from the Ramble* (1965), and *The Quest of the Gole* (1966). His forthcoming volume is *Types of Shape.*

Poems

of Our Moment

EDITED BY JOHN HOLLANDER

PEGASUS / NEW YORK

ACKNOWLEDGMENTS   We are indebted to and hereby thank the more than thirty pub-
lishers and agents who have granted us permission to reprint these poems:

By A. R. Ammons, "Corsons Inlet" and "The Misfit" from CORSONS INLET by A. R. Ammons,
copyright © 1965 by Cornell University Press, Ithaca, New York, and reprinted by
permission of Cornell University Press.
By John Ashbery, "Some Trees" and "The Picture of Little J. A. in a Prospect of Flowers"
from SOME TREES by John Ashbery, published by Yale University Press in 1956, copyright
© 1956 by John Ashbery, and reprinted by permission of John Ashbery, c/o Lynn
Nesbit, Marvin Josephson Associates, Inc., New York; "Rivers and Mountains" from
RIVERS AND MOUNTAINS by John Ashbery, copyright © 1962, 1963, 1964, 1966 by John
Ashbery, reprinted by permission of Holt, Rinehart and Winston, Inc., New York, and
from SELECTED POEMS by John Ashbery, reprinted by permission of Jonathan Cape, Ltd.,
London; "A Last World" from THE TENNIS COURT OATH by John Ashbery, copyright
© 1960 by John Ashbery, reprinted by permission of Wesleyan University Press, Mid-
dletown, Connecticut; "Definition of Blue" by courtesy of John Ashbery.

By Gregory Corso, "This Was My Meal" from GASOLINE, copyright © 1958 by Gregory Corso, reprinted by permission of City Lights Books, San Francisco; "Marriage" from THE HAPPY BIRTHDAY OF DEATH by Gregory Corso, copyright © 1960 by New Directions Publishing Corporation, New York, reprinted by their permission.

By Donald Davie, "Remembering the Thirties" from BRIDES OF REASON, published 1955 by Fantasy Press, Oxford, England; "A Winter Talent" and "Gardens No Emblems" from A WINTER TALENT, 1961, reprinted by permission of Routledge & Kegan Paul, Ltd., London; "The Hardness of Light," "Bolyai, the Geometer," "Low Lands," and "After an Accident" from EVENTS AND WISDOMS, copyright © 1965 by Donald Davie, reprinted by permission of Wesleyan University Press, Middletown, Connecticut, and Routledge & Kegan Paul, Ltd., London.

By Robert Dawson, "The Pigeon Roof" reprinted from SIX MILE CORNER by Robert Dawson with permission of Houghton Mifflin Company, Boston.

By James Dickey, "On the Hill Below the Lighthouse," "The Underground Stream," and "The Other," from INTO THE STONE by James Dickey, copyright 1957 by James Dickey; "Kudzu" and "Adultery" from HELMETS by James Dickey, and "Falling" from POEMS 1957–1967 by James Dickey, copyright © 1963 ("Kudzu") and 1966 ("Adultery" and "Falling") by James Dickey, reprinted by permission of Wesleyan University Press, Middletown, Connecticut, and Rapp & Carroll, Ltd., London; with special acknowledgment to *The New Yorker* magazine, in which "Kudzu," "Falling," and "The Underground Stream" first appeared.

By Alvin Feinman, "Preambles," "November Sunday Morning," "Landscape (Sicily)," "Pilgrim Heights," "Three Elementary Prophecies," and "Relic" from PREAMBLES AND OTHER POEMS by Alvin Feinman, copyright © 1964 by Alvin Feinman, reprinted by permission of Oxford University Press, New York.

By Allen Ginsberg, "Siesta in Xbalba and Return to the States" from REALITY SANDWICHES by Allen Ginsberg, copyright © 1963 by Allen Ginsberg; "America" and "A Supermarket in California" from HOWL by Allen Ginsberg, published 1956, copyright © 1967 by Allen Ginsberg, reprinted by permission of City Lights Books, San Francisco.

By Allen Grossman, "Husband and Wife" and "Lilith" from A HARLOT'S HIRE by Allen Grossman, published by Walker-DeBerry, Inc., Cambridge, 1961; "The Recluse" and "Tales of Odysseus" from THE RECLUSE by Allen Grossman, reprinted by courtesy of Allen Grossman.

By Thom Gunn, "Carnal Knowledge" from FIGHTING TERMS by Thom Gunn, first published 1954 by Fantasy Press, Oxford, England, and 1958 by Hawk's Well Press, New York; "On the Move," "The Corridor," and "Before the Carnival" from THE SENSE OF MOVEMENT by Thom Gunn, first published by The University of Chicago Press, 1957, are all reprinted by permission of Faber & Faber, Ltd., London; "Modes of Pleasure," "Black Jackets," and "My Sad Captains" from MY SAD CAPTAINS by Thom Gunn, copyright © 1961 by The University of Chicago Press; "Syon House," "Lebensraum," "Untitled Poem I," and "Untitled Poem II" from POSITIVES by Thom and Ander Gunn, copyright © 1966 by The University of Chicago Press, are reprinted by permission of The University of Chicago Press.

By Anthony Hecht, "La Condition Botanique," "Samuel Sewall," "The Dover Bitch," "The Origin of Centaurs," "The Vow," and "The Man Who Married Magdalene" from THE HARD HOURS by Anthony Hecht, published in 1967 by Atheneum House Inc., New York, reprinted by permission of the publisher. Copyright 1954, © 1957, 1960, 1961, 1967 by Anthony E. Hecht. "La Condition Botanique" and "Samuel Sewall" appeared in A SUMMONING OF STONES by Anthony Hecht; "The Dover Bitch" in *Transatlantic Review,* and the other three poems in *Hudson Review.* The last four poems are reprinted also by permission of Oxford University Press, London.

By Daryl Hine, "The Double-Goer," "Osiris Remembered," and "The Devil's Picture Book"

Copyright © 1965, 1966 by James Merrill. "The Broken Home" has appeared in *The New Yorker*, and "From the Cupola" in *Poetry*. "An Urban Convalescence" and "The Broken Home" are also reprinted by permission of Chatto & Windus, Ltd., London.

By W. S. Merwin, "White Goat, White Ram," copyright © 1956 by Alfred A. Knopf, Inc., reprinted from GREEN WITH BEASTS by W. S. Merwin, by permission of the publishers; "One-Eye" and "The Drunk in the Furnace" from THE DRUNK IN THE FURNACE by W. S. Merwin, copyright © 1958 by W. S. Merwin, published by Alfred A. Knopf, New York, and Rupert Hart-Davis, Ltd., London, reprinted by permission of Harold Ober Associates, Inc., New York, and David Higham Associates, Ltd., London; "The Way to the River" and "In the Night Fields" from THE MOVING TARGET, 1963, and "The Last One," "Some Last Questions," "Whenever I Go There," and "The River of Bees" from THE LICE by W. S. Merwin, 1967, both volumes published by Atheneum House, Inc., New York, reprinted by permission of Atheneum House, Inc., and David Higham Associates, Ltd., London.

By Frank O'Hara, "Poem: 'The eager note on my door . . .' " and "To the Harbormaster," copyright © 1957 by Frank O'Hara, from MEDITATIONS IN AN EMERGENCY by Frank O'Hara, reprinted by permission of Grove Press, Inc., New York; "Ode to Joy," copyright © 1958 by *Partisan Review*, New Brunswick, New Jersey, reprinted from Volume XXV, Number 3 (Summer 1958) with their permission; "Second Avenue," section 5, from SECOND AVENUE by Frank O'Hara, published by Corinth Books, New York, 1960, and reprinted by their permission; "Poem en Forme de Saw," copyright © 1964 by Frank O'Hara, reprinted from LUNCH POEMS by Frank O'Hara by permission of City Lights Books, San Francisco.

By Sylvia Plath, "The Bee Meeting," "The Arrival of the Bee Box," and "Death & Co.," copyright © 1963 by Ted Hughes, "The Night Dances," copyright © 1966 by Ted Hughes, from ARIEL by Sylvia Plath, reprinted by permission of Harper & Row, Publishers, New York, and Mr. Olwyn Hughes, London, Executor of the Estate of Sylvia Plath.

By Adrienne Rich, "Living in Sin" from THE DIAMOND CUTTERS, published by Harper & Row, New York, 1966, by courtesy of Adrienne Rich, New York; "The Roofwalker," "The Afterwake," "Juvenilia," "Rural Reflections," and "Peeling Onions," copyright © 1956, 1957, 1958, 1959, 1960, 1961, 1962, 1963, and 1967 by Adrienne Rich Conrad, from SNAPSHOTS OF A DAUGHTER-IN-LAW, reprinted by permission of W. W. Norton & Co., Inc., New York; "In the Woods," "The Trees," "Like This Together" and "Two Songs," copyright © 1966 by W. W. Norton & Company, from NECESSITIES OF LIFE by Adrienne Rich, reprinted by permission of W. W. Norton & Company, New York, and Chatto & Windus, Ltd., London.

By Frederick Seidel, "Wanting to Live in Harlem," copyright © 1962 by Frederick Seidel, from FINAL SOLUTIONS by Frederick Seidel, reprinted by permission of Random House, Inc., New York.

By David Shapiro, "The Will" and "First Love," copyright © 1962, 1963, 1964, and 1965 by David Shapiro, from JANUARY by David Shapiro, reprinted by permission of Holt, Rinehart and Winston, Inc., New York.

By Jon Silkin, "Death of a Son" and "Caring for Animals," copyright © 1954 by Jon Silkin, from THE PEACEABLE KINGDOM by Jon Silkin, "Furnished Lives," copyright © 1958 by Jon Silkin, from THE TWO FREEDOMS by Jon Silkin, "The Coldness," copyright 1961 by Jon Silkin, from THE RE-ORDERING OF THE STONES by Jon Silkin, "The Child" and "A Daisy," copyright © 1965 by Jon Silkin, from NATURE WITH MAN by Jon Silkin, all republished 1966 in POEMS, NEW AND SELECTED by Jon Silkin, and reprinted by permission of Wesleyan University Press, Middletown, Connecticut, and Chatto & Windus, Ltd., London.

Contents

Introduction

THIS COLLECTION contains work by thirty-four poets of the English language all of whom published their first volumes after 1950. Perhaps there is something arbitrary in so round a figure for use in mapping literary moments—it makes more sense to say that Wordsworth was nineteen in 1789 than that he was thirty at the turn of the nineteenth century, the twentieth century probably begins in England with the publication of the casualty lists from the battle of the Somme, and so forth. But other dates (the dropping of the Hiroshima bomb, Kennedy's assassination, the Suez crisis in England) may seem just as artificial, and boundaries are generally drawn in order to be pat, in any case. By 1950, the leading post-war poets of England and America had published their first volumes: Robert Lowell and Elizabeth Bishop; John Berryman (although with no obvious indications of how remarkable a turn his work would take with *Homage to Mistress Anne Bradstreet*); Richard Wilbur and Charles Olson had begun already to influence younger writers as polar instances of rhetorical closure and openness. In England, Philip Larkin had appeared on the scene, though Keith Douglas's first posthumous edition would not appear until the following year. William Empson's poetry had begun to be taken as seriously by poets as his criticism had been earlier. And in general, a transitional group of writers now stood between the younger poets of the post-war period and their teachers.

These teachers had their effects on many of these poets in various ways. Some, like John Crowe Ransom and Mark Van Doren, were there both as professors of literature in a formal way, and as serious attentive presences in a crucial and informal one. Some, like W. H. Auden and Robert Graves, were there in a more distant sense, to be read and, perhaps, visited. The generally enthusiastic encouragement of Canadian writers by Northrop Frye should be observed, too, as well as his more direct tutelage. I am not attempting to define a generation by its teachers so much as to suggest that a kind of relation to those teachers is indeed characteristic of a group of writers like this, only a handful of whom have ever taught, and less than a third of whom are currently attached to colleges and universities. While they were guided by poet-critics in the universities, relatively few of them are as committed critics as the generation of Ransom, Empson, Allen Tate and Robert Penn Warren, for example, had been. By the historical accident of his not having published a book of poems until his mid-forties, A. D. Hope is the one poet in this collection who stands, to Australian poetry certainly, in something like this relation; the astonishing perfection, too, of his adaptation of seventeenth-century poetry to timeless erotic concerns marks his significance as a master of some of the concerns of younger poets schooled in the doctrines of modernism. The youngest poet in this anthology has been to school, literally and figuratively, with some of the others in it. But I think it may be said of all the writers between these pages that their literary generation is marked by a feeling that it is not in the least peculiar for poetry to flourish in the buildings and grounds of the university. If cafes, barricades, trenches, garrets, and even offices have not yet become as mythical as their archetype, Parnassus, then they are at most temporary abodes.

In the selection of these poems, the editor has confronted all the usual anthologist's difficulties; the unending struggle between the claims of the representative and the distinctive, between the interests of the historical picture and the personally necessary, both show their results here. Even within the selection of poems by individual writers, personal dedication has not always permitted him to present the full shape of the career, however brief, in question. And there is no doubt that the current generation of poets is quite conscious of the problem of stylistic development, of the modulation of format, the rhetorical metamorphosis, the shift of moral focus—but above all, the constant problem of gaining better access to one's sources of imaginative power, those sources that the very pursuit of literature itself may cause to sink and narrow. If the almost melodramatic turn to the autobiographical in Robert Lowell's *Life Studies* (1959) produced some rather derivative results in the work of some younger writers, the more relevant analogue of such a change might be seen in the ways in which James Wright and W. S. Merwin have in recent years broken through the orderly syntax of their earlier poetry. They have evolved for themselves differingly new sorts of short poem, shaped and animated in the service of the images that demanded their presence. Or perhaps in the case of James Merrill's contrary formal motion toward the long poem and away from what might still be controlled by the highest form of epigram, or of John Ashbery's transcendence of an almost relentless experimentalism, seen in the very difficult poems of his second book, by a late rhetorical ease and formal beauty. In their different ways, all of these poets are engaged in the constant task of trying to be better as poets and, thereby, to get better as men.

But in some instances (as in that of Allen Ginsberg's early as opposed to his later work), a less programmatic principle of choice has been operating in this gathering of poems. Once the 1950 boundary, however unnatural, had been drawn (thus missing poets who are nevertheless very much with us in every sense, like Denise Levertov, Judith Wright in Australia, the Canadian James Reaney, etc.) the editor found that he was being motivated by that most immediate and fundamental of anthological principles: the desire to make certain poems keep company with each other and delight in the result. Under the rule of that principle certain necessary choices cannot but appear as idiosyncratic ones. Alvin Feinman, for example, may very well be the least known of the poets in this book; the editor, however, found his single book of verse to be an astonishing achievement and has chosen from it liberally. In any case, the kinds of pattern that might show up under more schematic choices are clearly in evidence here. The long poem, for instance, is evidenced by Allen Ginsberg's splendid *Siesta in Xbalba*, with its external theme of the power of vision to command one's return from it to the unceasingly actual; by James Merrill's transformation of the Cupid and Psyche story in *From the Cupola;* by the almost cinematic dislocations and transitions of James Dickey's recent *Falling;* and by the comedy and joy of Kenneth Koch's *Lunch*, that hymn to the imagination's banquet of sense eaten under the glistening of noon daylight. There is even the Mallarméan completeness of A. D. Hope's *The Double Looking Glass*, a treatment of the story of Susannah and the Elders whose meditative movement turns in a direction almost opposite to that of Stevens' *Peter Quince at the Clavier.*

Here, too, the reader will observe an uncalculated but inevitably necessary array of formal approaches to the problem of imaginative articulation. From Hope's unflaggingly true iambic quatrains (and the almost unmatched tour-de-force of his pentameter-tetrameter couplets in the seventeenth-century pastiche *Epistle*) to the phrasal fields of

A. R. Ammons' *Corsons Inlet*, the current poetic moment displays its range of metrical possibilities; generated by rhythm, syntax, image and tone, the structural forces of many modes of language lend their strength to incantation. From the many pitches of speech to the variety of inscriptions that overrun the contemporary urban forest, recent verse has drawn its aural and graphic cadences.

An anthology should perhaps always be open-ended, a continuing, self-revising collection that fulfills its hopes only in the very process of gathering—an editorial counterpart of the great unachievable Ode of the symbolists. But short of programming a computer to make an eternally changing selection of texts out of a vast number of possibles, size, cost, time, and taste unite to force a closure. In one instance, the poet himself refused permission for inclusion (Robert Duncan's *Poem Beginning With a Line By Pindar*). In the case of some other writers (Robert Creeley, for example), the right individual poems did not seem to present themselves.

In any event, this collection will be seen to represent our imaginative moment, whatever its duration is taken to be. While avoiding the specifically topical, these poems nevertheless respond in significant ways to the crises of institutional and cultural history which impinge on the imaginative consciousness of those who, like poets and painters (and maybe even mathematicians) build models *in*—and perhaps thereby *of*—reality. And whatever else they may achieve, these poems probably stand as some sort of testament to the continuing spiritual revolution to which poetry in English has been committed for more than a century-and-a-half, and to the ancillary struggle to redeem poetry itself, as the product of imaginative creation, from the sickness with which Literature as a realm is too often infected.

JOHN HOLLANDER
New York City
August, 1967

Poems

of Our Moment

A. R. Ammons

CORSONS INLET

I went for a walk over the dunes again this morning
to the sea,
then turned right along
    the surf

                rounded a naked headland
                and returned

    along the inlet shore:

it was muggy sunny, the wind from the sea steady and high,
crisp in the running sand,
    some breakthroughs of sun
  but after a bit

continuous overcast:

the walk liberating, I was released from forms,
from the perpendiculars,
    straight lines, blocks, boxes, binds
of thought
into the hues, shadings, rises, flowing bends and blends
        of sight:

                      I allow myself eddies of meaning:
yield to a direction of significance
running
like a stream through the geography of my work:
    you can find
in my sayings
           swerves of action
           like the inlet's cutting edge:

there are dunes of motion,
organizations of grass, white sandy paths of remembrance
in the overall wandering of mirroring mind:

but Overall is beyond me: is the sum of these events
I cannot draw, the ledger I cannot keep, the accounting
beyond the account:

in nature there are few sharp lines: there are areas of
primrose
        more or less dispersed;
disorderly orders of bayberry; between the rows
of dunes,
irregular swamps of reeds.
though not reeds alone, but grass, bayberry, yarrow, all . . .
predominantly reeds:

I have reached no conclusions, have erected no boundaries,
shutting out and shutting in, separating inside
        from outside: I have
        drawn no lines:
        as

manifold events of sand
change the dune's shape that will not be the same shape
tomorrow,

so I am willing to go along, to accept
the becoming
thought, to stake off no beginnings or ends, establish
        no walls:

by transitions the land falls from grassy dunes to creek
to undercreek: but there are no lines, though
        change in that transition is clear
        as any sharpness: but "sharpness" spread out,
allowed to occur over a wider range
than mental lines can keep:

the moon was full last night: today, low tide was low:
black shoals of mussels exposed to the risk
of air
and, earlier, of sun,
waved in and out with the waterline, waterline inexact,
caught always in the event of change:
a young mottled gull stood free on the shoals
and ate
to vomiting: another gull, squawking possession, cracked a crab,
picked out the entrails, swallowed the soft-shelled legs, a ruddy
turnstone running in to snatch leftover bits:

risk is full: every living thing in
siege: the demand is life, to keep life: the small
white blacklegged egret, how beautiful, quietly stalks and spears
the shallows, darts to shore
to stab—what? I couldn't
see against the black mudflats—a frightened
fiddler crab?

the news to my left over the dunes and
reeds and bayberry clumps was
fall: thousands of tree swallows
gathering for flight:
an order held
in constant change: a congregation
rich with entropy: nevertheless, separable, noticeable
as one event,
not chaos: preparations for
flight from winter,
cheet, cheet, cheet, cheet, wings rifling the green clumps,
beaks
at the bayberries:
a perception full of wind, flight, curve,
sound:
the possibility of rule as the sum of rulelessness:
the "field" of action
with moving, incalculable center:

in the smaller view, order tight with shape:
blue tiny flowers on a leafless weed: carapace of crab:
snailshell:
        pulsations of order
        in the bellies of minnows: orders swallowed,
broken down, transferred through membranes
to strengthen larger orders: but in the large view, no
lines or changeless shapes: the working in and out, together
      and against, of millions of events: this,
              so that I make
              no form of
              formlessness:

orders as summaries, as outcomes of actions override
or in some way result, not predictably (seeing me gain
the top of a dune,
the swallows
could take flight—some other fields of bayberry
        could enter fall
        berryless) and there is serenity:

        no arranged terror: no forcing of image, plan,
or thought:
no propaganda, no humbling of reality to precept:

terror pervades but is not arranged, all possibilities
of escape open: no route shut, except in
      the sudden loss of all routes:

        I see narrow orders, limited tightness, but will
not run to that easy victory:
        still around the looser, wider forces work:
        I will try
      to fasten into order enlarging grasps of disorder, widening
scope, but enjoying the freedom that
Scope eludes my grasp, that there is no finality of vision,
that I have perceived nothing completely,
        that tomorrow a new walk is a new walk.

THE MISFIT

The unassimilable fact leads us on:
round the edges
    where broken shapes make poor masonry
the synthesis
fails (and succeeds) into limitation
    or extending itself too far
becomes a different synthesis:
law applies
    consistently to the molecule,
not to the ocean, unoriented, unprocessed,
it floats in, that floats in it:
    we are led on

to the boundaries
where relations loosen into chaos
    or where the nucleus fails to control,
fragments in odd shapes
expressing more and more the interstitial sea:
    we are led on

to peripheries, to the raw blocks of material,
where mortar and trowel can convert
    diversity into enlarging unity:
not the million oriented facts
but the one or two facts,
    out of place,

recalcitrant, the one observed fact
that tears us into questioning:
    what has not
joined dies into order to redeem, with
loss of singleness extends the form,
    or, unassimilable, leads us on.

John Ashbery

SOME TREES

These are amazing: each
Joining a neighbour, as though speech
Were a still performance.
Arranging by chance

To meet as far this morning
From the world as agreeing
With it, you and I
Are suddenly what the trees try

To tell us we are:
That their merely being there
Means something; that soon
We may touch, love, explain.

And glad not to have invented
Such comeliness, we are surrounded:
A silence already filled with noises,
A canvas on which emerges

A chorus of smiles, a winter morning.
Placed in a puzzling light, and moving,
Our days put on such reticence
These accents seem their own defence.

THE PICTURE OF LITTLE J. A.
IN A PROSPECT OF FLOWERS

'He was spoilt from childhood by the future, which
he mastered rather early and apparently without
great difficulty.' —BORIS PASTERNAK

I

Darkness falls like a wet sponge
And Dick gives Genevieve a swift punch
In the pyjamas. 'Aroint thee, witch.'
Her tongue from previous ecstasy
Releases thoughts like little hats.

'He clap'd me first during the eclipse.
Afterwards I noted his manner
Much altered. But he sending
At that time certain handsome jewels
I durst not seem to take offence.'

In a far recess of summer
Monks are playing soccer.

II

So far is goodness a mere memory
Or naming of recent scenes of badness
That even these lives, children,
You may pass through to be blessed,
So fair does each invent his virtue.

And coming from a white world, music
Will sparkle at the lips of many who are
Beloved. Then these, as dirty handmaidens
To some transparent witch, will dream
Of a white hero's subtle wooing,
And time shall force a gift on each.

That beggar to whom you gave no cent
Striped the night with his strange descant.

III

Yet I cannot escape the picture
Of my small self in that bank of flowers:
My head among the blazing phlox
Seemed a pale and gigantic fungus.
I had a hard stare, accepting

Everything, taking nothing,
As though the rolled-up future might stink
As loud as stood the sick moment
The shutter clicked. Though I was wrong,
Still, as the loveliest feelings

Must soon find words, and these, yes,
Displace them, so I am not wrong
In calling this comic version of myself
The true one. For as change is horror,
Virtue is really stubbornness

And only in the light of lost words
Can we imagine our rewards.

A LAST WORLD

These wonderful things
Were planted on the surface of a round mind that was to become
    our present time.
The mark of things belongs to someone
But if that somebody was wise
Then the whole of things might be different
From what it was thought to be in the beginning, before an angel
    bandaged the field glasses.
Then one could say nothing hear nothing
Of what the great time spoke to its divisors.
All borders between men were closed.
Now all is different without having changed

As though one were to pass through the same street at different
    times
And nothing that is old can prefer the new.
An enormous merit has been placed on the head of all things
Which, bowing down, arrive near the region of their feet
So that the earth-stone has stared at them in memory at the
    approach of an error.
Still it is not too late for these things to die
Provided that an anemone will grab them and rush them to the
    wildest heaven.
But having plucked oneself, who could live in the sunlight?
And the truth is cold, as a giant's knee
Will seem cold.

Yet having once played with tawny truth
Having once looked at a cold mullet on a plate on a table
    supported by the weight of the inconstant universe
He wished to go far away from himself.
There were no baskets in those jovial pine-tree forests, and the waves
    pushed without whitecaps
In that foam where he wished to be.

Man is never without woman, the neuter sex
Casting up her equations, looks to her lord for loving kindness
For man smiles never at woman.
In the forests a night landslide could disclose that she smiled.
Guns were fired to discourage dogs into the interior
But woman—never. She is completely out of this world.
She climbs a tree to see if he is coming
Sunlight breaks at the edges of the wet lakes
And she is happy, if free
For the power he forces down at her like a storm of lightning.

Once a happy old man
One can never change the core of things, and light burns you the
    harder for it.
Glad of the changes already and if there are more it will never be
    you that minds
Since it will not be you to be changed, but in the evening in the
    severe lamplight doubts come

From many scattered distances, and do not come too near.
As it falls along the house, your treasure
Cries to the other men; the darkness will have none of you, and you
    are folded into it like mint into the sound of haying.
It was ninety-five years ago that you strolled in the serene little port;
    under an enormous cornice six boys in black slowly stood.
Six frock coats today, six black fungi tomorrow,
And the day after tomorrow—but the day after tomorrow itself is
    blackening dust.
You court obsidian pools
And from a tremendous height twilight falls like a stone and hits you.

You who were always in the way
Flower
Are you afraid of trembling like breath
But there is no breath in seriousness; the lake howls for it.
Swiftly sky covers earth, the wrong breast for a child to suck, and
    that,
What have you got there in your hand?
It is a stone.

So the passions are divided into tiniest units
And of these many are lost, and those that remain are given at
    nightfall to the uneasy old man
The old man who goes skipping along the roadbed.
In a dumb harvest
Passions are locked away, and states of creation are used instead,
    that is to say synonyms are used.

Honey
On the lips of elders is not contenting, so
A firebrand is made. Woman carries it,
She who thought herself good only for bearing children is decked out
    in the lace of fire
And this is exactly the way she wanted it, the trees coming to place
    themselves in her
In a rite of torpor, dust.
A bug carries the elixir
Naked men pray the ground and chew it with their hands

The fire lives
Men are nabbed
She her bonnet half off is sobbing there while the massacre yet
    continues with a terrific thin energy
A silver blaze calms the darkness.

Rest undisturbed on the dry of the beach
Flower
And night stand suddenly sideways to observe your bones
Vixen

Do men later go home
Because we wanted to travel
Under the kettle of trees
We thought the sky would melt to see us
But to tell the truth the air turned to smoke,
We were forced back onto a foul pillow that was another place.
Or were lost by our comrades
Somewhere between heaven and no place, and were growing smaller.
In another place a mysterious mist shot up like a wall, down which
    trickled the tears of our loved ones.
Bananas rotten with their ripeness hung from the leaves, and cakes
    and jewels covered the sand.
But these were not the best men
But there were moments of the others
Seen through indifference, only bare methods
But we can remember them and so we are saved.

A last world moves on the figures;
They are smaller than when we last saw them caring about them.
The sky is a giant rocking horse
And of the other things death is a new office building filled with
    modern furniture,
A wise thing, but which has no purpose for us.

Everything is being blown away;
A little horse trots up with a letter in its mouth, which is read with
    eagerness
As we gallop into the flame.

RIVERS AND MOUNTAINS

On the secret map the assassins
Cloistered, the Moon River was marked
Near the eighteen peaks and the city
Of humiliation and defeat—wan ending
Of the trail among dry, papery leaves
Gray-brown quills like thoughts
In the melodious but vast mass of today's
Writing through fields and swamps
Marked, on the map, with little bunches of weeds.
Certainly squirrels lived in the woods
But devastation and dull sleep still
Hung over the land, quelled
The rioters turned out of sleep in the peace of prisons
Singing on marble factory walls
Deaf consolation of minor tunes that pack
The air with heavy invisible rods
Pent in some sand valley from
Which only quiet walking ever instructs.
The bird flew over and
Sat—there was nothing else to do.
Do not mistake its silence for pride or strength
Or the waterfall for a harbor
Full of light boats that is there
Performing for thousands of people
In clothes some with places to go
Or games. Sometimes over the pillar
Of square stones its impact
Makes a light print.

So going around cities
To get to other places you found
It all on paper but the land
Was made of paper processed
To look like ferns, mud or other
Whose sea unrolled its magic

Distances and then rolled them up
Its secret was only a pocket
After all but some corners are darker
Than these moonless nights spent as on a raft
In the seclusion of a melody heard
As though through trees
And you can never ignite their touch
Long but there were homes
Flung far out near the asperities
Of a sharp, rocky pinnacle
And other collective places
Shadows of vineyards whose wine
Tasted of the forest floor
Fisheries and oyster beds
Tides under the pole
Seminaries of instruction, public
Places for electric light
And the major tax assessment area
Wrinkled on the plan
Of election to public office
Sixty-two years old bath and breakfast
The formal traffic, shadows
To make it not worth joining
After the ox had pulled away the cart.

Your plan was to separate the enemy into two groups
With the razor-edged mountains between.
It worked well on paper
But their camp had grown
To be the mountains and the map
Carefully peeled away and not torn
Was the light, a tender but tough bark
On everything. Fortunately the war was solved
In another way by isolating the two sections
Of the enemy's navy so that the mainland
Warded away the big floating ships.
Light bounced off the ends
Of the small gray waves to tell
Them in the observatory

About the great drama that was being won
To turn off the machinery
And quietly move among the rustic landscape
Scooping snow off the mountains rinsing
The coarser ones that love had
Slowly risen in the night to overflow
Wetting pillow and petal
Determined to place the letter
On the unassassinated president's desk
So that a stamp could reproduce all this
In detail, down to the last autumn leaf
And the affliction of June ride
Slowly out into the sun-blackened landscape.

DEFINITION OF BLUE

The rise of capitalism parallels the advance of romanticism
And the individual is dominant until the close of the nineteenth
    century.
In our own time, mass practices have sought to submerge the
    personality
By ignoring it, which has caused it instead to branch out in all
    directions
Far from the permanent tug that used to be its notion of "home."
These different impetuses are received from everywhere
And are as instantly snapped back, hitting through the cold
    atmosphere
In one steady, intense line.

There is no remedy for this "packaging" which has supplanted the
    old sensations.
Formerly there would have been architectural screens at the point
    where the action became most difficult
As a path trails off into shrubbery—confusing, forgotten, yet continuing
    to exist.
But today there is no point in looking to imaginative new methods

Since all of them are in constant use. The most that can be said for
     them further
Is that erosion produces a kind of dust or exaggerated pumice
Which fills space and transforms it, becoming a medium
In which it is possible to recognize oneself.

Each new diversion adds its accurate touch to the ensemble, and so
A portrait, smooth as glass, is built up out of multiple corrections
And it has no relation to the space or time in which it was lived.
Only its existence is a part of all being, and is therefore, I suppose,
     to be prized
Beyond chasms of night that fight us
By being hidden and present.

And yet it results in a downward motion, or rather a floating one
In which the blue surroundings drift slowly up and past you
To realize themselves some day, while you, in this nether world that
     could not be better
Waken each morning to the exact value of what you did and said,
     which remains.

Gregory Corso

THIS WAS MY MEAL

In the peas I saw upsidedown letters of MONK
And beside it, in the Eyestares of Wine
I saw Olive & Blackhair
   I decided sunset to dine

I cut through the cowbrain and saw Christmas
& my birthday run hand in hand in the snow
I cut deeper
   and Christmas bled to the edge of the plate

I turned to my father
   and he ate my birthday
I drank my milk and saw trees outrun themselves
   valleys outdo themselves
     and no mountain stood a chance of not walking

Desert came in the spindly hands of stepmother
I wanted to drop fire-engines from my mouth!
But in ran the moonlight and grabbed the prunes.

MARRIAGE

Should I get married? Should I be good?
Astound the girl next door with my velvet suit and faustus hood?
Don't take her to movies but to cemeteries
tell all about werewolf bathtubs and forked clarinets
then desire her and kiss her and all the preliminaries
and she going just so far and I understanding why
not getting angry saying You must feel! It's beautiful to feel!

Instead take her in my arms lean against an old crooked tombstone
and woo her the entire night the constellations in the sky—

When she introduces me to her parents
back straightened, hair finally combed, strangled by a tie,
should I sit knees together on their 3rd degree sofa
and not ask Where's the bathroom?
How else to feel other than I am,
often thinking Flash Gordon soap—
O how terrible it must be for a young man
seated before a family and the family thinking
We never saw him before! He wants our Mary Lou!
After tea and homemade cookies they ask What do you do for a
                                                       living?
Should I tell them? Would they like me then?
Say All right get married, we're losing a daughter
but we're gaining a son—
And should I then ask Where's the bathroom?

O God, and the wedding! All her family and her friends
and only a handful of mine all scroungy and bearded
just wait to get at the drinks and food—
And the priest! he looking at me as if I masturbated
asking me Do you take this woman for your lawful wedded wife?
And I trembling what to say say Pie Glue!
I kiss the bride all those corny men slapping me on the back
She's all yours, boy! Ha-ha-ha!
And in their eyes you could see some obscene honeymoon going on—
Then all that absurd rice and clanky cans and shoes
Niagara Falls! Hordes of us! Husbands! Wives! Flowers! Chocolates!
All streaming into cozy hotels
All going to do the same thing tonight
The indifferent clerk he knowing what was going to happen
The lobby zombies they knowing what
The whistling elevator man he knowing
The winking bellboy knowing
Everybody knowing! I'd be almost inclined not to do anything!
Stay up all night! Stare that hotel clerk in the eye!
Screaming: I deny honeymoon! I deny honeymoon!

running rampant into those almost climactic suites
yelling Radio belly! Cat shovel!
O I'd live in Niagara forever! in a dark cave beneath the Falls
I'd sit there the Mad Honeymooner
devising ways to break marriages, a scourge of bigamy
a saint of divorce—

But I should get married I should be good
How nice it'd be to come home to her
and sit by the fireplace and she in the kitchen
aproned young and lovely wanting my baby
and so happy about me she burns the roast beef
and comes crying to me and I get up from my big papa chair
saying Christmas teeth! Radiant brains! Apple deaf!
God what a husband I'd make! Yes, I should get married!
So much to do! like sneaking into Mr Jones' house late at night
and cover his golf clubs with 1920 Norwegian books
Like hanging a picture of Rimbaud on the lawnmower
like pasting Tannu Tuva postage stamps all over the picket fence
like when Mrs Kindhead comes to collect for the Community Chest
grab her and tell her There are unfavorable omens in the sky!
And when the mayor comes to get my vote tell him
When are you going to stop people killing whales!
And when the milkman comes leave him a note in the bottle
Penguin dust, bring me penguin dust, I want penguin dust—

Yet if I should get married and it's Connecticut and snow
and she gives birth to a child and I am sleepless, worn,
up for nights, head bowed against a quiet window, the past behind
me,
finding myself in the most common of situations a trembling man
knowledged with responsibility not twig-smear nor Roman coin soup—
O what would that be like!
Surely I'd give it for a nipple a rubber Tacitus
For a rattle a bag of broken Bach records
Tack Della Francesca all over its crib
Sew the Greek alphabet on its bib
And build for its playpen a roofless Parthenon

No, I doubt I'd be that kind of father
not rural not snow no quiet window
but hot smelly tight New York City
seven flights up, roaches and rats in the walls
a fat Reichian wife screeching over potatoes Get a job!
And five nose running brats in love with Batman
and the neighbors all toothless and dry haired
like those hag masses of the 18th century
all wanting to come in and watch TV
The landlord wants his rent
Grocery store Blue Cross Gas & Electric Knights of Columbus
Impossible to lie back and dream Telephone snow, ghost parking—
No! I should not get married I should never get married!
But—imagine If I were married to a beautiful sophisticated woman
tall and pale wearing an elegant black dress and long black gloves
holding a cigarette holder in one hand and a highball in the other
and we lived high up in a penthouse with a huge window
from which we could see all of New York and ever farther on
                                                    clearer days
No, can't imagine myself married to that pleasant prison dream—

O but what about love! I forget love
not that I am incapable of love
it's just that I see love as odd as wearing shoes—
I never wanted to marry a girl who was like my mother
And Ingrid Bergman was always impossible
And there's maybe a girl now but she's already married
And I don't like men and—
but there's got to be somebody!
Because what if I'm 60 years old and not married,
all alone in a furnished room with pee stains on my underwear
and everybody else is married! All the universe married but me!

Ah, yet well I know that were a woman possible as I am possible
then marriage would be possible—
Like SHE in her lonely alien gaud waiting her Egyptian lover
so I wait—bereft of 2,000 years and the bath of life.

Donald Davie

REMEMBERING THE THIRTIES

1

Hearing one saga, we enact the next.
We please our elders when we sit enthralled;
But then they're puzzled; and at last they're vexed
To have their youth so avidly recalled.

It dawns upon the veterans after all
That what for them were agonies, for us
Are highbrow thrillers, though historical;
And all their feats quite strictly fabulous.

This novel written fifteen years ago,
Set in my boyhood and my boyhood home,
These poems about "abandoned workings" show
Worlds more remote than Ithaca or Rome.

The Anschluss, Guernica—all the names
At which those poets thrilled or were afraid
For me mean schools and schoolmasters and games;
And in the process some one is betrayed.

Ourselves perhaps. The Devil for a joke
Might carve his own initials on our desk,
And yet we'd miss the point because he spoke
An idiom too dated, Audenesque.

Ralegh's Guiana also killed his son.
A pretty pickle if we came to see
The tallest story really packed a gun,
The Telemachiad an Odyssey.

2

Even to them the tales were not so true
As not to be ridiculous as well:
The ironmaster met his Waterloo,
But Rider Haggard rode along the fell.

"Leave for Cape Wrath tonight!" They lounged away
On Fleming's trek or Isherwood's ascent.
England expected every man that day
To show his motives were ambivalent.

They played the fool, not to appear as fools
In time's long glass. A deprecating air
Disarmed, they thought, the jeers of later schools;
Yet irony itself is doctrinaire,

And, curiously, nothing now betrays
Their type to time's derision like this coy
Insistence on the quizzical, their craze
For showing Hector was a mother's boy.

A neutral tone is nowadays preferred.
And yet it may be better, if we must,
To find the stance impressive and absurd
Than not to see the hero for the dust.

For courage is the vegetable king,
The sprig of all ontologies, the weed
That beards the slag-heap with his hectoring,
Whose green adventure is to run to seed.

A WINTER TALENT

Lighting a spill late in the afternoon,
I am that coal whose heat it should unfix;

Winter is come again, and none too soon
For meditation on its raft of sticks.

Some quick bright talents can dispense with coals
And burn their boats continually, command
An unreflecting brightness that unrolls
Out of whatever firings come to hand.

What though less sunny spirits never turn
The dry detritus of an August hill
To dangerous glory? Better still to burn
Upon that gloom where all have felt a chill.

GARDENS NO EMBLEMS

Man with a scythe: the torrent of his swing
Finds its own level, and is not hauled back
But gathers fluently, like water rising
Behind the watergates that close a lock.

The gardener eased his foot into a boot;
Which action like the mower's had its mould,
Being itself a sort of taking root,
Feeling for lodgment in the leather's fold.

But forms of thought move in another plane
Whose matrices no natural forms afford
Unless subjected to prodigious strain:
Say, light proceeding edgewise, like a sword.

THE HARDNESS OF LIGHT

'Via Portello,' I wrote,
'The fruity garbage-heaps . . .'
As if someone had read my poems,

Padua eight years later
Is so hot no one sleeps.

But this is a different quarter,
Just off the *autostrada,*
Touched by that wand of transit,
Californian, hopeful . . .
I grow older, harder.

I wake in the night, to rain.
All the old stench released
On the risen night wind carries
Coolness across the city,
Streaming from west to east.

The equivocal breath of change,
In a clatter of sudden slats
Across the room, disturbs me
More than ever, in new
Motels and blocks of flats.

What is this abomination
When a long hot spell is breaking?
Sour smell of my own relief?
The rankness of cooling-off?
Rottenness of forsaking?

I glare. In that renowned
Hard light of burning skies
Nothing grows durable
With age. It neither solves
Nor even simplifies.

BOLYAI, THE GEOMETER

Arthur Allen, when he lived
In rooms beneath my rooms in Trinity,

Thought he had made a breakthrough that would turn
Mathematics inside out again,

As once geometry was spun around
Because the non-Euclidean emerged
Not out of nature, out of nothing extant
But simply as imaginable. Shade,

A flap of blackness folded back upon
Pillar and pediment that afternoon
Encroached upon the chapel portico
And there a wing whirled, flashing. So, I thought,

This turning inside-out is not so hard:
One looks across Front Square and there it is,
A wing that whirls white undersides, sustained
By what endangers it, the press of air.

And though his torque was different, not in nature,
And though my science is as pure as his,
Knowing no revolution more profound
Than that from black on white to white on black

(As though a shutter shot across the mind
One sees the lately formless as most formal,
The stanza most a unit when
Open at both ends, all transition) still

How pure is mathematics? Not enough
For Farkas Bolyai: 'Not geometry
Is altogether pure. This is a wound
Large and perpetual upon my soul.'

So with poetics: never a revolution
But has its mould. Look, in the overturning
Approaching comber, rolling inside out,
A roof of cream moves back through a mounting wall.

LOW LANDS

I could not live here, though I must and do
Ungratefully inhabit the Cambridgeshire fens
And the low river delta we pass through
Is beautiful in the same uncertain sense.

Like a snake it is, its serpentine iridescence
Of slow light spilt and wheeling over calm
Inundations, and a snake's still menace
Hooding with bruised sky belfry and lonely farm.

The grasses wave on meadows fat with foison.
In granges, cellars, granaries, the rat
Runs sleek and lissom. Tedium, a poison,
Swells in the sac for the hillborn, dwelling in the flat.

How defenceless it is! How much it needs a protector
To keep its dykes! At what a price it commands
The delightful bizarre when it wears like a bus-conductor
Tickets of brown sails tucked into polders' hat-bands!

But a beauty there is, noble, dependent, unshrinking,
In being at somebody's mercy, wide and alone.
I imagine a hillborn sculptor suddenly thinking
One could live well in a country short of stone.

AFTER AN ACCIDENT

I

Smashed, and brought up against
Last things like pines'
Steep shadows and the purple
Hole in my darling's head,

I recall as an amulet
Against my shallowness
Uncalculated kindness
So much! Death, in my dream,

Half-length as in a portrait,
Cocks his eye, leads mine
Up a toothbrush ridge of pines
With an amused complicity

At seeing what is so
Beneath us as a mountain
Tower above us when
We have run out of road.

Death is about my age,
Smiling and dark, clean-shaven.
Behind him the valley-floor
Is ledged in a purple light.

Had I not sought the shade
Of what is so
Beneath us as chagrin,
I had not been afraid

Of his mountainous purple light,
Nor should I have run out
Of the soul of gratitude
Before I ran out of death.

II. BETWEEN DEAD AND ALIVE

For you to be thinking how
It was no bad place to lie in,
In this there was nothing morbid;
Nor was it too composed
In me, to think of your dying
As of an emigration.

This century one in five
On that hillside has emigrated,
And this is not melancholy,
Nor the spaciousness disconcerting:
Between the dead and alive
The ratio there is a just one.

And yet I would have sworn
Such thoughts as these were tricks
Of tearful literature;
That thoughts so unresentful
As mine were could not mix
With terror and compunction.

III. THE HEARTLAND

And so it is clear that this
Heartland has to be painted
In unrepresentative colours;

That the forests under the mountains
Live in an orange light
Without reference to sunset.

How clear it is, and how
Incapable of being
Foreseen or offered as solace,

That remorse without regret
Is a possible state of the soul,
Like grief without resentment.

IV. THE WINDFALL

So Death is what one day
You have run out of, like
Luck or a bank-balance.
In that case, what is
Coming into it like?

Like coming into money!
The death we run out of is
Not the life we run out of;
The death that we may
With luck come into, is.

And without money, life
Is not worth living.
How did you manage
All these years,
Living and not living?

V. THANKS

You never did so much
As when you nearly died;
As if you nearly died
That I might show I lived.

That was no more your motive
Than it could have been my choice.
You cannot think I live
Just to give voice!

It was no poet's need you met,
And now survive,
But the need I had as a man
To know myself alive.

You never did so much
As when you nearly died;
You had to nearly die
For me to know I lived.

Robert Dawson

THE PIGEON ROOF

The speaker is a high school student in California.

Science. The flapping flight of birds
like the flight of this my poem to its destination
straight though ruffling the surfaces of many ponds

frets my waking. Those honking personalists,
Canada geese? No, the coo of lecherous pigeons,
plum breasts thudding transom and gable, spoils

the small dawn of my bedroom. Whose eyelids
scrape the cornea like pigeon toes? it is
the march hare physicist, the ultimate masochist,

that from braying beasts flays hide with thumb-
triggered bombs. Not pleasant to wake with dreams
if not to wake is not escaping too. Her shoes last night

skinned the dashboard, who slapped me when I turned
the speaker out. Manifolds, gaskets. Flutter valves?
Something I thought of hearts. Behind the screen

a hill sulks. Betraying the car to the checker of cars
by yellow green aisle lights ordered, till we saw
projectors flicker, blown tints sliding into shapes unseen,

we climbed. A damp rock scabbed with moss, black
between feathers of black, live oaks and manzanita,
an arbitrary island. Somewhere the swinging glass doors

of St. Luke's Emergency were nothing of the moment.

Planes crooned over us. Raid horns we heard or didn't hear,
no history being except in torment of made things.

Pecked slate rifts and the sky drips blue?
Mathematical beams and cross beams loft me in silence.
Linoleum curls my toes and gives me away.

Five years I sleep here under the pigeon roof.
Once I shall wake and be myself. This poem
to relate my later by my former scenes.

Of art. The young man nailed to his page,
whose back the nurse screws higher, is death's
cautious lover. Capillaries pop and the white cells

swim the tendons. Plastic hawsers moor him to us living.
Red strings gurgle in his elbow pits. His scrawl falls
and smacks a fan and the interns scoop it, smooth it

on linen low across his chest, so birdcage thin a poem
stabs water. Weeks of relapse. Three of us filched
winesaps that we dove for in the orchard ditch. Chocolate

ripples roiled us toward the pumps, which drank us? Each
time just in time bare flanks raked waiting fingers on the
escarpment. Two, in his attic pestered by maps and pennants,

perched on cartons of Safeway encyclopedias, traded verses.
Chianti bloodied his shirt cuff. He whispered starry drunks
his heroes flung . . . My lines ran short but he held out

till dawn. The nurse excludes me when his mother comes.
Not right to meddle with his dying so. The page I drop
before I go says death's a method. Time through time I cry

don't read it! don't! my time is now! that youth
whose forty swinish selves grunt pity, change to me!
Released, he tramps a golf course, snacks, and faints.

Gray wings sort currents north in spring. Blue bitterns,
pouters, bobwhites and the hermit thrush. From granite bluffs
I cast sardines for plovers. The surf-line sings as the bird

wheels deep. No one fishes this shore of the ocean. No
one ties together these things in a bunch.
I listen to my blood roar in a conch.

This beach is splintered with the homes of crawling things.
He dies while I'm a thousand miles and here.
At dawn the drive-in screen is yellow blue and rust.

Of history. Braceros pitch their own dirt with the tents.
Ma and me picked hop flowers once. Her fingers itched
And bloodied in the dew. I picked too small. They

canned us. Three who know each other only as he drives,
commuters, ride another's tailgate through a fog. Stalled
on a grade an oil truck. Later we fished their bodies with a torch.

Plum and emerald goiters, pigeons strut these caves, that glut
on popcorn daylong on the courthouse lawn. White squab
filthy the plaster laths, or if they hatch dead, packrats

stitch their eyes? This attic no one visits from the quake.
Old man my father splints the trapdoor with a crow. Not
clear who enters, but with cardboard blinds the roof's

false windows, mornings crystallized. Bell-beats on the
shingles. What flies first shatters its beak on a rafter.
Powder and pellets yellow our legs. Some amateur's fled

tumbler somersaults when clubbed and drops an egg. Shovels,
brooms. Hundreds of wings sheer off in flags or fractured
skate their own dirt buffeting. I cross my hands so the wrist

bones crackle. Blood glues their wrung skulls in your palms
while feathers flurry smoke. Cedar apples hiss. Bluejays
pester a squirrel. Cones and yellow needles bed a cigarette.

Smoke vines from bough up redwood bough. An owl glides
by the fire trail, his wingtips dripping flame? Parachutes
fouled in a barranca shred on juniper. So long as any

timber grows, the fire must, dry groves and cherry stones.
Then gobble the prairies. Even the tide burns. Ripples
from what sank here churn higher as they spread.

Without me seconds pass. If in the mind mind
is structured, wattled in some nest, its history creates
one unity for who would flee or fight.

—For Delbert Pedgrift

James Dickey

ON THE HILL BELOW THE LIGHTHOUSE

Now I can be sure of my sleep;
I have lost the blue sea in my eyelids.
From a place in the mind too deep
For thought, a light like a wind is beginning.
Now I can be sure of my sleep.

When the moon is held strongly within it,
The eye of the mind opens gladly.
Day changes to dark, and is bright,
And miracles trust to the body,
When the moon is held strongly within it.

A woman comes true when I think her.
Her eyes on the window are closing.
She has dressed the stark wood of a chair.
Her form and my body are facing.
A woman comes true when I think her.

Shade swings, and she lies against me.
The lighthouse has opened its brain.
A browed light travels the sea.
Her clothes on the chair spread their wings.
Shade swings, and she lies against me.

Let us lie in returning light,
As a bright arm sweeps through the moon.
The sun is dead, thinking of night
Swung round like a thing on a chain.
Let us lie in returning light.

Let us lie where your angel is walking

In shadow, from wall onto wall,
Cast forth from your off-cast clothing
To pace the dim room where we fell.
    Let us lie where your angel is walking,

Coming back, coming back, going over.
An arm turns the light world around
The dark. Again we are waiting to hover
In a blaze in the mind like a wind
    Coming back, coming back, going over.

    Now I can be sure of my sleep;
    The moon is held strongly within it.
    A woman comes true when I think her.
    Shade swings, and she lies against me.
    Let us lie in returning light;
    Let us lie where your angel is walking,
    Coming back, coming back, going over.

THE UNDERGROUND STREAM

I lay at the edge of a well,
And thought how to bury my smile
Under the thorn, where the leaf,
At the sill of oblivion safe,
Put forth its instant green
In a flow from underground.
I sought how the spirit could fall
Down this moss-feathered well:
The motion by which my face
Could descend through structureless grass,
Dreaming of love, and pass
Through solid earth, to rest
On the unseen water's breast,
Timelessly smiling, and free
Of the world, of light, and of me.
I made and imagined that smile

To float there, mile on mile
Of streaming, unknowable wonder,
Overhearing a silence like thunder
Possess every stone of the well
Forever, where my face fell
From the upper, springtime world,
And my odd, living mouth unfurled
An eternal grin, while I
In the bright and stunned grass lay
And turned to air without age.
My first love fingered a page
And sang with Campion.
The heart in my breast turned green;
I entered the words afresh,
At one with her singing flesh.
But all the time I felt
The secret triumph melt
Down through the rooted thorn,
And the smile I filtered through stone
Motionless lie, not murmuring
But listening only, and hearing
My image of joy flow down.
I turned from the girl I had found
In a song once sung by my mother,
And loved my one true brother,
The tall cadaver, who
Either grew or did not grow,
But smiled, with the smile of singing,
Or a smile of incredible longing
To rise through a circle of stone,
Gazing up at a sky, alone
Visible, at the top of a well,
And seeking for years to deliver
His mouth from the endless river
Of my oil-on-the-water smile,
And claim his own grave face
That mine might live in its place.
I lay at the edge of a well;
And then I smiled, and fell.

THE OTHER

Holding onto myself by the hand,
I change places into the spirit
I had as a rack-ribbed child,
And walk slowly out through my mind
To the wood, as into a falling fire
Where I turned from that strength-haunted body
Half-way to bronze, as I wished to:

Where I slung up the too-heavy ax-head
And prayed to my thunderous ear-drums
That the deep sweat fall with the leaves
And raise up a man's shape upon me,
Come forth from the work of my arms
And the great, dead tree I hit down on:
That the chicken-chested form I belabored

Might swell with the breast of a statue
From out of the worm-shattered bole,
While I talked all the time through my teeth
To another, unlike me, beside me:
To a brother or king-sized shadow
Who looked at me, burned, and believed me:
Who believed I would rise like Apollo

With armor-cast shoulders upon me:
Whose voice, whistling back through my teeth,
Counted strokes with the hiss of a serpent.
Where the sun through the bright wood drove
Him, mute, and floating strangely, to the ground,
He led me into his house, and sat
Upright, with a face I could never imagine,

With a great harp leant on his shoulder,
And began in deep handfuls to play it:
A sail strung up on its spirit

Gathered up in a ruin in his arms,
That the dog-tired soul might sing
Of the hero, withheld by its body,
Upsprung like a magical man

To a dying, autumnal sound.
As I stood in the shadow-ruled clearing,
Wind died, all over a thicket.
Leaves stood everywhere within falling,
And I thought of our taking the harp
To the tree I had battered to pieces
Many times, many days, in a fever,

With my slow-motion, moon-sided ax.
Reason fell from my mind at a touch
Of the cords, and the dead tree leapt
From the ground, and together, and alive.
I thought of my body to come;
My mind burst into that green.
My brother rose beside me from the earth,

With the wing-bone of music on his back
Trembling strongly with heartfelt gold,
And ascended like a bird into the tree,
And music fell in a comb, as I stood
In a bull's heavy, bronze-bodied shape
As it mixed with a god's, on the ground,
And leaned on the helve of the ax.

Now, owing my arms to the dead
Tree, and the leaf-loosing, mortal wood,
Still hearing that music amaze me,
I walk through the time-stricken forest,
And wish another body for my life,
Knowing that none is given
By the giant, unusable tree

And the leaf-shapen lightning of sun,
And rail at my lust of self

With an effort like chopping through root-stocks:
Yet the light, looming brother but more
Brightly above me is blazing,
In that music come down from the branches
In utter, unseasonable glory.

Telling nothing but how I made
By hand, a creature to keep me dying
Years longer, and coming to sing in the wood
Of what love still might give,
Could I turn wholly mortal in my mind,
My body-building angel give me rest,
This tree cast down its foliage with the years.

KUDZU

Japan invades. Far Eastern vines
Run from the clay banks they are

Supposed to keep from eroding,
Up telephone poles,
Which rear, half out of leafage,
As though they would shriek,
Like things smothered by their own
Green, mindless, unkillable ghosts.
In Georgia, the legend says
That you must close your windows

At night to keep it out of the house.
The glass is tinged with green, even so,

As the tendrils crawl over the fields.
The night the kudzu has
Your pasture, you sleep like the dead.
Silence has grown Oriental
And you cannot step upon ground:
Your leg plunges somewhere

It should not, it never should be,
Disappears, and waits to be struck

Anywhere between sole and kneecap:
For when the kudzu comes,

The snakes do, and weave themselves
Among its lengthening vines,
Their spade heads resting on leaves,
Growing also, in earthly power
And the huge circumstance of concealment.
One by one the cows stumble in,
Drooling a hot green froth,
And die, seeing the wood of their stalls

Strain to break into leaf.
In your closed house, with the vine
Tapping your window like lightning,
You remember what tactics to use.
In the wrong, yellow fog-light of dawn
You herd them in, the hogs,
Head down in their hairy fat,
The meaty troops, to the pasture.
The leaves of the kudzu quake
With the serpents' fear, inside

The meadow ringed with men
Holding sticks, on the country roads.

The hogs disappear in the leaves.
The sound is intense, subhuman,
Nearly human with purposive rage.
There is no terror
Sound from the snakes.
No one can see the desperate, futile
Striking under the leaf heads.
Now and then, the flash of a long

Living vine, a cold belly,

Leaps up, torn apart, then falls
Under the tussling surface.
You have won, and wait for frost,
When, at the merest touch
Of cold, the kudzu turns
Black, withers inward and dies,
Leaving a mass of brown strings
Like the wires of a gigantic switchboard.
You open your windows,

With the lightning restored to the sky
And no leaves rising to bury

You alive inside your frail house,
And you think, in the opened cold,
Of the surface of things and its terrors,
And of the mistaken, mortal
Arrogance of the snakes
As the vines, growing insanely, sent
Great powers into their bodies
And the freedom to strike without warning:

From them, though they killed
Your cattle, such energy also flowed

To you from the knee-high meadow
(It was as though you had
A green sword twined among
The veins of your growing right arm—
Such strength as you would not believe
If you stood alone in a proper
Shaved field among your safe cows—):
Came in through your closed

Leafy windows and almighty sleep
And prospered, till rooted out.

ADULTERY

We have all been in rooms
We cannot die in, and they are odd places, and sad.
Often Indians are standing eagle-armed on hills

In the sunrise   open wide to the Great Spirit
Or gliding in canoes   or cattle are browsing on the walls
Far away   gazing down with the eyes of our children

Not far away   or there are men driving
The last railspike, which has turned
Gold in their hands. Gigantic forepleasure lives

Among such scenes, and we are alone with it
At last. There is always some weeping
Between us   and someone is always checking

A wrist watch by the bed to see how much
Longer we have left. Nothing can come
Of this   nothing can come

Of us: of me with my grim techniques
Or you who have sealed your womb
With a ring of convulsive rubber:

Although we come together,
Nothing will come of us. But we would not give
It up, for death is beaten

By praying Indians   by distant cows   historical
Hammers   by hazardous meetings that bridge
A continent. One could never die here

Never die   never die
While crying. My lover, my dear one
I will see you next week

When I'm in town. I will call you
If I can. Please get hold of   please don't
Oh God, Please don't any more I can't bear . . . Listen:

We have done it again   we are
Still living. Sit up and smile,
God bless you. Guilt is magical.

FALLING

A 29-year-old stewardess fell . . . to her
death tonight when she was swept
through an emergency door that sud-
denly sprang open . . . The body . . .
was found . . . three hours after the
accident. —NEW YORK TIMES

The states when they black out and lie there rolling   when they
    turn
To something transcontinental   move by   drawing moonlight out
    of the great
One-sided stone hung off the starboard wingtip   some sleeper next to
An engine is groaning for coffee   and there is faintly coming in
Somewhere the vast beast-whistle of space. In the galley with its racks
Of trays   she rummages for a blanket   and moves in her slim
    tailored
Uniform to pin it over the cry at the top of the door. As though she
    blew

The door down with a silent blast from her lungs   frozen   she is
    black
Out finding herself   with the plane nowhere and her body taking
    by the throat
The undying cry of the void   falling   living   beginning to be
    something
That no one has ever been and lived through   screaming without
    enough air

Still neat   lipsticked   stockinged   girdled by regulation   her
    hat
Still on   her arms and legs in no world   and yet spaced also
    strangely
With utter placid rightness on thin air   taking her time   she holds
    it
In many places   and now, still thousands of feet from her death
    she seems
To slow   she develops interest   she turns in her maneuverable
    body

To watch it. She is hung high up in the overwhelming middle of
    things in her
Self   in low body-whistling wrapped intensely   in all her dark
    dance-weight
Coming down from a marvellous leap   with the delaying,
    dumfounding ease
Of a dream of being drawn   like endless moonlight to the harvest
    soil
Of a central state of one's country   with a great gradual warmth
    coming
Over her   floating   finding more and more breath in what she has
    been using
For breath   as the levels become more human   seeing clouds
    placed honestly
Below her left and right   riding slowly toward them   she clasps
    it all
To her and can hang her hands and feet in it in peculiar ways   and
Her eyes opened wide by wind, can open her mouth as wide   wider
    and suck
All the heat from the cornfields   can go down on her back with a
    feeling
Of stupendous pillows stacked under her   and can turn   turn as
    to someone
In bed   smile, understood in darkness   can go away   slant
    slide
Off tumbling   into the emblem of a bird with its wings half-spread
Or whirl madly on herself   in endless gymnastics in the growing
    warmth

Of wheatfields rising toward the harvest moon.   There is time to live
In superhuman health   seeing mortal unreachable lights far down
    seeing
An ultimate highway with one late priceless car probing it   arriving
In a square town   and off her starboard arm the glitter of water
    catches
The moon by its one shaken side   scaled, roaming silver   My God
    it is good
And evil   lying in one after another of all the positions for love
Making   dancing   sleeping   and now cloud wisps at her no
Raincoat   no matter   all small towns brokenly brighter from
    inside
Cloud   she walks over them like rain   bursts out to behold a
    Greyhound
Bus shooting light through its sides   it is the signal to go straight
Down like a glorious diver   then feet first   her skirt stripped
    beautifully
Up   her face in fear-scented cloths   her legs deliriously bare
    then
Arms out   she slow-rolls over   steadies out   waits for something
    great
To take control of her   trembles near feathers   planes head-down
The quick movements of bird-necks turning her head   gold eyes
    the insight-
eyesight of owls blazing into the hencoops   a taste for chicken
    overwhelming
Her   the long-range vision of hawks enlarging all human lights
    of cars
Freight trains   looped bridges   enlarging the moon racing slowly
Through all the curves of a river   all the darks of the midwest
    blazing
From above. A rabbit in a bush turns white   the smothering
    chickens
Huddle   for over them there is still time for something to live
With the streaming half-idea of a long stoop   a hurtling   a fall
That is controlled   that plummets as it wills   turns gravity
Into a new condition, showing its other side like a moon   shining
New Powers   there is still time to live on a breath made of nothing
But the whole night   time for her to remember to arrange her skirt

Like a diagram of a bat   tightly it guides her   she has this
      flying-skin
Made of garments   and there are also those sky-divers on TV
      sailing
In sunlight   smiling under their goggles   swapping batons back
      and forth
And He who jumped without a chute and was handed one by a diving
Buddy. She looks for her grinning companion   white teeth
      nowhere
She is screaming   singing hymns   her thin human wings spread
      out
From her neat shoulders   the air beast-crooning to her   warbling
And she can no longer behold the huge partial form of the world
      now
She is watching her country lose its evoked master shape   watching
      it lose
And gain   get back its houses and peoples   watching it bring up
Its local lights   single homes   lamps on barn roofs   if she fell
Into water she might live   like a diver   cleaving   perfect
      plunge

Into another   heavy silver   unbreathable   slowing   saving
Element: there is water   there is time to perfect all the fine
Points of diving   feet together   toes pointed   hands shaped
      right
To insert her into water like a needle   to come out healthily
      dripping
And be handed a Coca-Cola   there they are   there are the waters
Of life   the moon packed and coiled in a reservoir   so let me
      begin
To plane across the night air of Kansas   opening my eyes
      superhumanly
Bright   to the dammed moon   opening the natural wings of my
      jacket
By Don Loper   moving like a hunting owl toward the glitter of
      water
One cannot just *fall   just tumble screaming all that time   one*
      must use

It   she is now through with all   through all   clouds   damp
          hair
Straightened   the last wisp of fog pulled apart on her face like wool
          revealing
New darks   new progressions of headlights along dirt roads from
          chaos

And night   a gradual warming   a new-made, inevitable world of
          one's own
Country   a great stone of light in its waiting waters   hold   hold
          out
For water: who knows when what correct young woman must take
          up her body
And fly   and head for the moon-crazed inner eye of midwest
          imprisoned
Water   stored up for her for years   the arms of her jacket slipping
Air up her sleeves to go   all over her? What final things can be
          said
Of one who starts out sheerly in her body in the high middle of night
Air   to track down water like a rabbit where it lies like life itself
Off to the right in Kansas? She goes toward   the blazing bare lake
Her skirts neat   her hands and face warmed more and more by the
          air
Rising from pastures of beans   and under her   under chenille
          bedspreads
The farm girls are feeling the goddess in them struggle and rise
          brooding
On the scratch-shining posts of the bed   dreaming of female signs
Of the moon   male blood like iron   of what is really said by the
          moan
Of airliners passing over them at dead of midwest midnight   passing
Over brush fires   burning out in silence on little hills   and will
          wake
To see the woman they should be   struggling on the rooftree to
          become
Stars: for her the ground is closer   water is nearer   she passes
It   then banks   turns   her sleeves fluttering differently as she
          rolls

Out to face the east, where the sun shall come up from wheatfields
          she must
Do something with water   fly to it   fall in it   drink it   rise
From it   but there is none left upon earth   the clouds have drunk
          it back
The plants have sucked it down   there are standing toward her only
The common fields of death   she comes back from flying to falling
Returns to a powerful cry   the silent scream with which she blew
          down
The coupled door of the airliner   nearly   nearly losing hold
Of what she has done   remembers   remembers the shape at the
          heart
Of cloud   fashionably swirling   remembers she still has time to die
Beyond explanation. Let her now take off her hat in summer air the
          contour
Of cornfields   and have enough time to kick off her one remaining
Shoe with the toes   of the other foot   to unhook her stockings
With calm fingers, noting how fatally easy it is to undress in midair
Near death   when the body will assume without effort any position
Except the one that will sustain it   enable it to rise   live
Not die   nine farms hover close   widen   eight of them separate,
          leaving
One in the middle   then the fields of that farm do the same   there
          is no
Way to back off   from her chosen ground   but she sheds the jacket
With its silver sad impotent wings   sheds the bat's guiding tailpiece
Of her skirt   the lightning-charged clinging of her blouse   the
          intimate
Inner flying-garment of her slip in which she rides like the holy
          ghost
Of a virgin   sheds the long windsocks of her stockings   absurd
Brassiere   then feels the girdle required by regulations squirming
Off her: no longer monobuttocked   she feels the girdle flutter
          shake
In her hand   and float   upward   her clothes rising off her
          ascending
Into cloud   and fights away from her head the last sharp dangerous
          shoe

Like a dumb bird   and now will drop in   SOON   now will dro

In like this   the greatest thing that ever came to Kansas   dow
    from all
Heights   all levels of American breath   layered in the lungs
    from the frail
Chill of space to the loam where extinction slumbers in corn tasse
    thickly
And breathes like rich farmers counting: will come among them afte
Her last superhuman act   the last slow careful passing of her hand
All over her unharmed body   desired by every sleeper in his dream
Boys finding for the first time their loins filled with heart's blood
Widowed farmers whose hands float under light covers to find
    themselves
Arisen at sunrise   the splendid position of blood unearthly draw
Toward clouds   all feel something   pass over them as she passe
Her palms over *her* long legs   *her* small breasts   and deeply
    between
Her thighs   her hair shot loose from all pins   streaming in th
    wind
Of her body   let her come openly   trying at the last second to lan
On her back   This is it   THIS
                                All those who find her impresse
In the soft loam   gone down   driven well into the image of he
    body
The furrows for miles flowing in upon her where she lies very dee
In her mortal outline   in the earth as it is in cloud   can tell
    nothing
But that she is there   inexplicable   unquestionable   and
    remember
That something broke in them as well   and began to live and di
    more
When they walked for no reason into their fields to where the whol
    earth
Caught her   interrupted her maiden flight   told her how to li
    she cannot
Turn   go away   cannot move   cannot slide off it and assum
    another

Position   no sky-diver with any grin could save her   hold her in
     his arms
Plummet with her   unfold above her his wedding silks   she can no
     longer
Mark the rain with whirling women that take the place of a dead wife
Or the goddess in Norwegian farm girls   or all the back-breaking
     whores
Of Wichita. All the known air above her is not giving up quite one
Breath   it is all gone   and yet not dead   not anywhere else
Quite   lying still in the field on her back   sensing the smells
Of incessant growth try to lift her   a little sight left in the corner
Of one eye   fading   seeing something wave   lies believing
That she could have made it   at the best part of her brief goddess
State   to water   gone in headfirst   come out smiling
     invulnerable
Girl in a bathing-suit ad   but she is lying like a sunbather at the
     last
Of moonlight   half-buried in her impact on the earth   not far
From a railroad trestle   a water tank   she could see if she could
Raise her head from her modest hole   with her clothes beginning
To come down all over Kansas   into bushes   on the dewy sixth
     green
Of a golf course   one shoe   her girdle coming down fantastically
On a clothesline, where it belongs   her blouse on a lightning rod:

Lies in the fields   in *this* field   on her broken back as though on
A cloud she cannot drop through   while farmers sleepwalk without
Their women from houses   a walk like falling toward the far waters
Of life   in moonlight   toward the dreamed eternal meaning of
     their farms
Toward the flowering of the harvest in their hands   that tragic cost
Feels herself go   go toward   go outward   breathes at last fully
Not   and tries   less   once   tries   tries   AH, GOD—

Alvin Feinman

PREAMBLES

I

Vagrant, back, my scrutinies
The candid deformations as with use
A coat or trousers of one now dead
Or as habit smacks of certitude

Even cosmographies, broad orchards
The uncountable trees   Or a river
Seen along the green monotonies
Of its banks   And the talk

Of memorable ideals ending
In irrelevance   I would cite
Wind-twisted spaces, absence
Listing to a broken wall

And the cornered noons
Our lives played in, such things
As thwart beginnings, limit   Or
Juxtapose that longest vision

A bright bird winged to its idea
To the hand stripped
By a damaged resolution
Daily of its powers   *Archai*

Bruited through crumbling masteries
To hang like swollen apples
In the river, witnesses
Stilled to their clotted truth   All

Discursion fated and inept
So the superior reality
Of photographs   The soul's
Tragic abhorrence of detail.

II

Only, if then, the ordered state
The storied sentiment of rest
Of the child hand in the father's
Rigored, islands tethered

To complicit seas, and tempering
Winds to lull the will
To evidence, to the ripe profit
Of perfections, gardens

Rhyming the space we walk in
Harmony of season and design   So
Statues hold through every light
The grave persuasive

Candors of their stride   And so
The mind in everything it joins
And suffers to redeem apart
Plays victim to its own intent

Divines generics blooded
To its needs   The sculptor
Lending outward in his stroke
To each defeat a signature

The just reconnaissance
That even fruit, each excellence
Confirms its course   A leisure
As of sap or blood arrested

Only once and to the prime
Its issue vivifies   A sun

Luring the divisioned calms
The days extended under it.

III

But only loosed or salient
Out of this unbinding stream
The stain of dyings seen
On pavements and on blurted

Slopes of ground   As there
Where your farthest reach
Is lived of want or membership
The ranged and slackened traffics

Cease   A bird in mid-flight
Falls, let silence, hair
The credible of touch adventure
There   Or certain laughters

Freedoms and the heat
Of only arms and of the thighs
These even love's rejoinder
As of every severed thing

The *ecce* only, only hands
Or hardnesses, the gleam a water
Or a light, a paused thing
Clothes in vacua killed

To a limbless beauty   Take
These torn possessives there
Where you plead the radiant
Of your truth's gloom   Own

To your sleep, your waking
The tread that is walked
From the inner of its pace
The play of a leaf to an earth.

NOVEMBER SUNDAY MORNING

And the light, a wakened heyday of air
Tuned low and clear and wide,
A radiance now that would emblaze
And veil the most golden horn
Or any entering to a sudden clearing
To a standing, astonished, revealed . . .

That the actual streets I loitered in
Lay lit like fields, or narrow channels
About to open to a burning river;
All brick and window vivid and calm
As though composed in a rigid water
No random traffic would dispel . . .

As now through the park, and across
The chill nailed colors of the roofs,
And on near trees stripped bare,
Corrected in the scant remaining leaf
To their severe essential elegance,
Light is the all-exacting good,

That dry, forever, virile stream
That wipes each thing to what it is,
The whole, collage and stone, cleansed
To its proper pastoral . . .
                                        I sit
And smoke, and linger out desire.

LANDSCAPE (SICILY)

I have seen your steeples and your lands
Speared by awkward cactuses and long birds

Flatten your yellow stones, your worn mountains.

Surely where those hills spilled villages
Toward the sea I should have wanted
Savagery, a touch icier than physical sport;

But vegetation withered from a forest
Of inconclusive starts, memory only
Gathered to a shade in the sun-sorrowed square.

A shade, sun-struck, whose hold will cover
The play of boys in blood-red clothing
And call your seasons to a wall of flatted rhythms,

To a slow summit of retreating days, days
Like winds through given linen, through dust.
These green reductions of your ancient freedoms—

The stunted olive, the lizard fixed
In soundless grasses, your yellow stones
Rubbed by the moon, the moon-quelled beaches,

And all asceticisms grown separate, skilled
To plump intrinsic endings—the fig-tree's
Sudden, rounded fingers; history

At the close will cripple to these things:
A body without eyes, a hand, the vacant
Presence of unjoined, necessary things.

PILGRIM HEIGHTS

Something, something, the heart here
Misses, something it knows it needs
Unable to bless—the wind passes;
A swifter shadow sweeps the reeds,
The heart a colder contrast brushes.

So this fool, face-forward, belly
Pressed among the rushes, plays out
His pulse to the dune's long slant
Down from blue to bluer element,
The bold encompassing drink of air

And namelessness, a length compound
Of want and oneness the shore's mumbling
Distantly tells—something a wing's
Dry pivot stresses, carved
Through barrens of stillness and glare:

The naked close of light in light,
Light's spare embrace of blade and tremor
Stealing the generous eye's plunder
Like a breathing banished from the lung's
Fever, lost in parenthetic air.

Raiding these nude recesses, the hawk
Resumes his yielding balance, his shadow
Swims the field, the sands beyond,
The narrow edges fed out to light,
To the sea's eternal licking monochrome.

The foolish hip, the elbow bruise
Upright from the dampening mat,
The twisted grasses turn, unthatch,
Light-headed blood renews its stammer—
Apart, below, the dazed eye catches

A darkened figure abruptly measured
Where folding breakers lay their whites;
The heart from its height starts downward,
Swum in that perfect pleasure
It knows it needs, unable to bless.

THREE ELEMENTARY PROPHECIES

1. For Departure

You will not want what gives this going speech
Only as loss the stay of it
Not the rhythm drained into its sense
Like a world surviving

Only as absence, as a silence touched
A thing out of the body gone, desire
Or a blood-accustomed dread

Nor seek a knowledge of this breach
A name of it, as love
The flawless metamorphosis of dying
Stilled to its idea

Or membered like presentiment or choice
To your days' held mine
A sentence, or the letter of a truth

Only this presence destined
As a weather from its source
Toward broad or violent unleashings
Fables of the suffered and the joined

The rest unnumbered and devoid
A wind that will not move or pass
Rain tangled to a ruin, to
A season's felled forgotten root.

2. For Passage

Think then the ruin of your thoughts, and where
The persistent blood beats still under them,
Of birds you cannot follow with your eye.

Think the dark and breeding thickets
Where lowly animals die, and over the gloom
Bright birds passing in the light:

"What is your life if not the flashed stroke
Of your meaning, of water
Hurled once or blindly against rock,

Your living laid to the pillow of its sleep
As windows close to the street's tumult,
To love's long minute and the lips . . ."

Nail your will to the yellow fallings
Of your days, as tragedies slip
Their herald warnings through their acts.

Own land and sky, all seeing suffering things,
Water riding water, wing and roof,
The rip and baggage of all your ways.

3. For Return

Far, the farthest exile, and the steed
You ride must paw the ground, riderless,
Death's resignation come to matter

To mercies walked from the same blue fulcrum
Where your powers impel you
Unobscured by necessary pities,
                                    hungers
Come like numbered birds in the common air
And needs before they improvise their names

There love will touch where your energies begin
Where your hand asks you light from primary colors,
Assembles a mystery detained by sorrows

Like roofs the color of particular houses

And the logic of unexpected trees, love
Like sons will be far in the night
Close, as horses in the night, and welcome.

RELIC

I will see her stand
half a step back of the edge of some high place
or at a leafless tree in some city park
or seated with her knees toward me and her face
      turned toward the window

And always the tips of the fingers of both her hands
will pull or twist at a handkerchief
like lovely deadly birds at a living thing
trying to work apart something exquisitely,
      unreasonably joined.

Allen Ginsberg

AMERICA

America I've given you all and now I'm nothing.
America two dollars and twentyseven cents January 17, 1956.
I can't stand on my own mind.
America when will we end the human war?
Go fuck yourself with your atom bomb.
I don't feel good don't bother me.
I won't write my poem till I'm in my right mind.
America when will you be angelic?
When will you take off your clothes?
When will you look at yourself through the grave?
When will you be worthy of your million Trotskyites?
America why are your libraries full of tears?
America when will you send your eggs to India?
I'm sick of your insane demands.
When can I go into the supermarket and buy what I need with my
     good looks?
America after all it is you and I who are perfect not the next world.
Your machinery is too much for me.
You made me want to be a saint.
There must be some other way to settle this argument.
Burroughs is in Tangiers I don't think he'll come back it's sinister.
Are you being sinister or is this some form of practical joke?
I'm trying to come to the point.
I refuse to give up my obsession.
America stop pushing I know what I'm doing.
America the plum blossoms are falling.
I haven't read the newspapers for months, everyday somebody goes
     on trial for murder.
America I feel sentimental about the Wobblies.
America I used to be a communist when I was a kid I'm not sorry.

I smoke marijuana every chance I get.

I sit in my house for days on end and stare at the roses in the closet.

When I go to Chinatown I get drunk and never get laid.

My mind is made up there's going to be trouble.

You should have seen me reading Marx.

My psychoanalyst thinks I'm perfectly right.

I won't say the Lord's Prayer.

I have mystical visions and cosmic vibrations.

America I still haven't told you what you did to Uncle Max after he
    came over from Russia.

I'm addressing you.

Are you going to let your emotional life be run by Time Magazine?

I'm obsessed by Time Magazine.

I read it every week.

Its cover stares at me every time I slink past the corner candystore.

I read it in the basement of the Berkeley Public Library.

It's always telling me about responsibility. Businessmen are serious.
    Movie producers are serious. Everybody's serious but me.

It occurs to me that I am America.

I am talking to myself again.

Asia is rising against me.

I haven't got a chinaman's chance.

I'd better consider my national resources.

My national resources consist of two joints of marijuana millions of
    genitals an unpublishable private literature that goes 1400
    miles an hour and twentyfive-thousand mental institutions.

I say nothing about my prisons nor the millions of underprivileged
    who live in my flowerpots under the light of five hundred suns.

I have abolished the whorehouses of France, Tangiers is the next to
    go.

My ambition is to be President despite the fact that I'm a Catholic.

America how can I write a holy litany in your silly mood?

I will continue like Henry Ford my strophes are as individual as
    his automobiles more so they're all different sexes.

America I will sell you strophes $2500 apiece $500 down on your
    old strophe

America free Tom Mooney
America save the Spanish Loyalists
America Sacco & Vanzetti must not die
America I am the Scottsboro boys.
America when I was seven momma took me to Communist Cell
     meetings they sold us garbanzos a handful per ticket
     a ticket costs a nickel and the speeches were free
     everybody was angelic and sentimental about the workers
     it was all so sincere you have no idea what a good thing
     the party was in 1835 Scott Nearing was a grand old man
     a real mensch Mother Bloor made me cry I once saw
     Israel Amter plain. Everybody must have been a spy.
America you don't really want to go to war.
America it's them bad Russians.
Them Russians them Russians and them Chinamen. And them
     Russians.
The Russia wants to eat us alive. The Russia's power mad. She
     wants to take our cars from out our garages.
Her wants to grab Chicago. Her needs a Red Readers' Digest. Her
     wants our auto plants in Siberia. Him big bureaucracy run-
     ning our fillingstations.

That no good. Ugh. Him make Indians learn read. Him need big
     black niggers. Hah. Her make us all work sixteen hours a
     day. Help.
America this is quite serious.
America this is the impression I get from looking in the television
     set.
America is this correct?
I'd better get right down to the job.
It's true I don't want to join the Army or turn lathes in precision
     parts factories, I'm nearsighted and psychopathic anyway.
America I'm putting my queer shoulder to the wheel.

A SUPERMARKET IN CALIFORNIA

What thoughts I have of you tonight, Walt Whitman, for I walked down the sidestreets under the trees with a headache self-conscious looking at the full moon.

In my hungry fatigue, and shopping for images, I went into the neon fruit supermarket, dreaming of your enumerations!

What peaches and what penumbras! Whole families shopping at night! Aisles full of husbands! Wives in the avocados, babies in the tomatoes!—and you, Garcia Lorca, what were you doing down by the watermelons?

I saw you, Walt Whitman, childless, lonely old grubber, poking among the meats in the refrigerator and eyeing the grocery boys.

I heard you asking questions of each: Who killed the pork chops? What price bananas? Are you my Angel?

I wandered in and out of the brilliant stacks of cans following you, and followed in my imagination by the store detective.

We strode down the open corridors together in our solitary fancy tasting artichokes, possessing every frozen delicacy, and never passing the cashier.

Where are we going, Walt Whitman? The doors close in an hour. Which way does your beard point tonight?

(I touch your book and dream of our odyssey in the supermarket and feel absurd.)

Will we walk all night through solitary streets? The trees add shade to shade, lights out in the houses, we'll both be lonely.

Will we stroll dreaming of the lost America of love past blue automobiles in driveways, home to our silent cottage?

Ah, dear father, graybeard, lonely old courage-teacher, what America did you have when Charon quit poling his ferry and you got out on a smoking bank and stood watching the boat disappear on the black waters of Lethe?

SIESTA IN XBALBA
AND RETURN TO THE STATES

dedicated to Karena Shields

I

Late sun opening the book,
            blank page like light,
invisible words unscrawled,
            impossible syntax
of apocalypse—
            Uxmal: Noble Ruins
No construction—

            let the mind fall down.

—One could pass valuable months
and years perhaps a lifetime
doing nothing but lying in a hammock
reading prose with the white doves
            copulating underneath
and monkeys barking in the interior
            of the mountain
and I have succumbed to this
            temptation—

'They go mad in the Selva—'
            the madmen read
and laughed in his hammock

            eyes watching me:
unease not of the jungle
            the poor dear,
can tire one—
            all that mud

and all those bugs . . .
       ugh. . . .

Dreaming back I saw
an eternal kodachrome
souvenir of a gathering
of souls at a party,
crowded in an oval flash:
cigarettes, suggestions,
laughter in drunkenness,
broken sweet conversation,
acquaintance in the halls,
faces posed together,
stylized gestures,
odd familiar visages
and singular recognitions
that registered indifferent
greeting across time:
Ansen reading Horace
with a rolling head,
white-handed Hohnsbean
camping gravely
with an absent glance,
bald Kingsland drinking
out of a huge glass,
Dusty in a party dress,
Durgin in white shoes
gesturing from a chair,
Keck in a corner waiting
for subterranean music,
Helen Parker lifting
her hands in surprise:
all posturing in one frame,
superficially gay
or tragic as may be,
illumed with the fatal
character and intelligent
actions of their lives.

And I in a concrete room
    above the abandoned
labyrinth of Palenque
    measuring my fate,
wandering solitary in the wild
    —blinking singleminded
at a bleak idea—
    until exhausted with
its action and contemplation
    my soul might shatter
at one primal moment's
    sensation of the vast
movement of divinity.

As I leaned against a tree
    inside the forest
expiring of self-begotten love,
I looked up at the stars absently,
    as if looking for
something else in the blue night
    through the boughs,
and for a moment saw myself
    leaning against a tree . . .

. . . back there the noise of a great party
    in the apartments of New York,
half-created paintings on the walls, fame,
    cocksucking and tears,
money and arguments of great affairs,
    the culture of my generation . . .

    my own crude night imaginings,
my own crude soul notes taken down
    in moments of isolation, dreams,
piercings, sequences of nocturnal thought
    and primitive illuminations

—uncanny feeling the white cat
    sleeping on the table

will open its eyes in a moment
        and be looking at me—.

One might sit in this Chiapas
recording the apparitions in the field
        visible from a hammock
looking out across the shadow of the pasture
in all the semblance of Eternity

        . . . a dwarfed thatch roof
down in the grass in a hollow slope
under the tall crowd of vegetation
        waiting at the wild edge:
the long shade of the mountain beyond
        in the near distance,
its individual hairline of trees
traced fine and dark along the ridge

        against the transparent sky light,
rifts and holes in the blue air
        and amber brightenings of clouds
disappearing down the other side
        into the South . . .

        palms with lethargic feelers
rattling in presage of rain,
        shifting their fronds
in the direction of the balmy wind,
        monstrous animals
sprayed up out of the ground
        settling and unsettling
as in water . . .
        and later in the night
a moment of premonition
when the plenilunar cloudfilled sky
        is still and small.

So spent a night

with drug and hammock
at Chichen Itza on the Castle:—

I can see the moon
moving over the edge of the night forest
and follow its destination
through the clear dimensions of the sky
from end to end of the dark
circular horizon.

High dim stone portals,
entablatures of illegible scripture,
bas-reliefs of unknown perceptions:
and now the flicker of my lamp
and smell of kerosene on dust-
strewn floor where ant wends
its nightly ritual way toward great faces
worn down by rain.
In front of me a deathshead
half a thousand years old
—and have seen cocks a thousand
old grown over with moss and batshit
stuck out of the wall
in a dripping vaulted house of rock—
but deathshead's here
on portal still and thinks its way
through centuries the thought
of the same night in which I sit
in skully meditation
—sat in many times before by
artisan other than me
until his image of ghostly change
appeared unalterable—
but now his fine thought's vaguer
than my dream of him:
and only the crude skull figurement's
gaunt insensible glare is left,
with its broken plumes of sensation

and indecipherable headdresses of intellect
                    scattered in the madness of oblivion
to holes and notes of elemental stone,
blind face of animal transcendency
                    over the holy ruin of the world
dissolving into the sunless wall of a blackened room
                    on a time-rude pyramid rebuilt
                    in the bleak flat night of Yucatan
where I come with my own mad mind to study
                    alien hieroglyphs of Eternity.

A creak in the rooms scared me.

Some sort of bird, vampire or swallow,
                    flees with little paper wingflap
around the summit in its own air unconcerned
                    with the great stone tree I perch on.

                    Continual metallic
whirr of chicharras,
                    then lesser chirps
of cricket: 5 blasts
                    of the leg whistle.
The creak of an opening
                    door in the forest,
some sort of weird birdsong
                    or reptile croak.

My hat woven of hennequin
                    on the stone floor
as a leaf on the waters,
                    as perishable;
my candle wavers continuously
                    and will go out.

Pale Uxmal,
                    unhistoric, like a dream,
Tuluum shimmering on the coast in ruins;
Chichen Itza naked

constructed on a plain;
Palenque, broken chapels in the green
basement of a mount;
lone Kabah by the highway;
Piedras Negras buried again
by dark archaeologists;
Yaxchilan
resurrected in the wild,
and all the limbo of Xbalba still unknown—

floors under roofcomb of branch,
foundation to ornament
tumbled to the flowers,
pyramids and stairways
raced with vine,
limestone corbels
down in the river of trees,
pillars and corridors
sunken under the flood of years:

Time's slow wall overtopping
all that firmament of mind,
as if a shining waterfall of leaves and rain
were built down solid from the endless sky
through which no thought can pass.

A great red fat rooster
mounted on a tree stump
in the green afternoon,
the ego of the very fields,
screams in the holy sunlight!

—I can't think with that
supersonic cock intensity
crucifying my skull
in its imaginary sleep.

—was looking back
with eyes shut to

where they crawled
like ants on brown old temples
building their minute ruins
and disappearing into the wild
leaving many mysteries
of deathly volition
to be divined.

I alone know the great crystal door
to the House of Night,
a legend of centuries
—I and a few Indians.

And had I mules and money I could find
the Cave of Amber
and the Cave of Gold
rumored of the cliffs of Tumbala.

I found the face of one
of the Nine Guardians of the Night
hidden in a mahogany hut
in the Area of Lost Souls
—first relic of kind for that place.

And I found as well a green leaf
shaped like a human heart;
but to whom shall I send this
anachronistic valentine?

Yet these ruins so much
woke me to nostalgia
for the classic stations
of the earth,
the ancient continent
I have not seen
and the few years
of memory left
before the ultimate night
of war.

As if these ruins were not enough,
                as if man could go
no further before heaven
                till he exhausted
the physical round
                of his own mortality
in the obscure cities
                hidden in the ageing world

. . . the few actual
                ecstatic conscious souls
certain to be found,
                familiars . . .
returning after years
                to my own scene
transfigured:
                to hurry change
to hurry the years
                bring me to my fate.

So I dream nightly of an embarcation,
                captains, captains,
iron passageways, cabin lights,
                Brooklyn across the waters,
the great dull boat, visitors, farewells,
                the blurred vast sea—
one trip a lifetime's loss or gain:

as Europe is my own imagination
                —many shall see her,
                many shall not—
though it's only the old familiar world
and not some abstract mystical dream.

And in a moment of previsioning sleep
                I see that continent in rain,
black streets, old night, a
                fading monument . . .

And a long journey unaccomplished
        yet, on antique seas
rolling in gray barren dunes under
        the world's waste of light
toward ports of childish geography
        the rusty ship will
harbor in . . .

What nights might I not see
        penniless among the Arab
mysteries of dirty towns around
        the casbahs of the docks?
Clay paths, mud walls,
        the smell of green cigarettes,
creosote and rank salt water—
        dark structures overhead,
shapes of machinery and façade
        of hull: and a bar lamp
burning in the wooden shack
        across from the dim
mountain of sulphur on the pier.

        Toward what city
will I travel? What wild houses
        do I go to occupy?
What vagrant rooms and streets
        and lights in the long night
urge my expectation? What genius
        of sensation in ancient
halls? what jazz beyond jazz
        in future blue saloons?
what love in the cafes of God?

I thought, five years ago
        sitting in my apartment,
my eyes were opened for an hour
        seeing in dreadful ecstasy
the motionless buildings

      of New York rotting
under the tides of Heaven.

There is a god
dying in America
already created
in the imagination of men
made palpable
for adoration:
there is an inner
anterior image
of divinity
beckoning me out
to pilgrimage.

O future, unimaginable God.

> Finca Tacalapan de San
> Leandro, Palenque,
> Chiapas, Mexico 1954—
> San Francisco 1955

II

Jump in time
      to the immediate future,
another poem:

      return to the old land
penniless and with
      a disconnected manuscript,
the recollection of a few
      sensations, beginning:

logboat down Rio Michol
      under plantain
and drifting trees
      to the railroad,

darkness on the sea
looking toward the stations
of the classic world—

another image descending
in white mist
down the lunar highway
at dawn, above
Lake Catemaco on the bus
—it woke me up—
the far away likeness
of a heavenly file
of female saints
stepping upward
on miniature arches
of a gold stairway
into the starry sky,
the thousands of little
saintesses in blue hoods
looking out at me
and beckoning:
SALVATION!
It's true,
simple as in the image.

Then the mummies
in their Pantheon
at Guanajuato—
a city of Cortesian
mines in the first
crevasse of the Sierras,
where I rested—

for I longed to see their
faces before I left:
these weren't mythical rock
images, tho stone
—limestone effigies out
of the grave, remains

of the fatal character—

newly resurrected,
           grasping their bodies
with stiff arms, in soiled
           funeral clothes;
twisted, knock-kneed,
           like burning
screaming lawyers—
what hallucinations
           of the nerves?—
indecipherable-sexed;
           one death-man had
raised up his arms
           to cover his eyes,
significant timeless
           reflex in sepulchre:

apparitions of immortality
           consumed inward,
waiting openmouthed
           in the fireless darkness.
Nearby, stacked symmetrically,
           a skullbone wall ending
the whitewashed corridor
           under the graveyard
—foetid smell reminiscent
           of sperm and drunkenness—
the skulls empty and fragile,
           numerous as shells,
—so much life passed through
           this town . . .

The problem is isolation
           —there in the grave
or here in oblivion of light.

           Of eternity we have
a numbered score of years

and fewer tender moments
—one moment of tenderness
and a year of intelligence
and nerves: one moment of pure
bodily tenderness—
I could dismiss Allen with grim
pleasure.

Reminder: I knelt in my room
on the patio at San Miguel
at the keyhole: 2 A.M.
The old woman lit a candle.
Two young men and their girls
waited before the portal,
news from the street. She
changed the linen, smiling.

What joy! The nakedness!
They dance! They talk
and simper before the door,
they lean on a leg,
hand on a hip, and posture,
nudity in their hearts,
they clap a hand to head
and whirl and enter,
pushing each other,
happily, happily,
to a moment of love . . .

What solitude I've
finally inherited.

Afterward fifteen hours
on rubbled single lane,
broken bus rocking along
the maws and continental crags
of mountain afternoon,
the distant valleys fading,
regnant peaks beyond

to days on the Pacific
         where I bathed

then riding, fitful,
         gazing, sleeping
through the desert
         beside a wetback
sad-faced old-man-
         youth, exhausted
to Mexicali

         to stand
near one night's dark shack
         on the garbage cliffs
of bordertown overhanging
         the tin house poor
man's village below,
         a last night's
timewracked brooding
         and farewell,
the end of a trip.

—Returning
         armed with New Testament,
critic of horse and mule,
         tanned and bearded
satisfying Whitman, concerned
         with a few Traditions,
metrical, mystical, manly
. . . and certain characteristic flaws

         —enough!
The nation over the border
grinds its arms and dreams
         of war: I see
the fiery blue clash
         of metal wheels
clanking in the industries
         of night, and

detonation of infernal bombs

        . . . and the silent downtown
of the States
        in watery dusk submersion.

Guanajuato—Los Angeles, 195

[NOTE: Uxmal and other proper names mentioned in the first part of the poem are those of ruined cities. Xbalba, translatable as morning Star in Region Obscure, or Hope, and pronounced Chivalvá, is the area in Chiapas between the Tobasco border and the Usumascintla River at the edge of the Peten Rain Forest; the boundary of lower Mexico and Guatemala today is thereabouts. The locale was considered a Purgatory or Limbo, the legend is vague, in the (Old) Mayan Empire. To the large tree at the crest of what is now called Mount Don Juan, at the foot of which this poem was written, ancient craftsmen came to complete work left unfinished at their death.]

Allen Grossman

HUSBAND AND WIFE

In late July when all the early flowers
Were quite spent and spring with its joy was gone
The day grew cloudy toward the afternoon.
At last we could not say the sun had set
Or that it had not. Without sight of the sky
We speculated on the time of day
Like perpetual workers underground
Or like the learned, or blind, or like two lovers.
I said, being the man I was,
"Lest the gorgeous sunset be forgot
I will presume to rise above the clouds
And see the sun go down," and yet I could not,
Being the man I was, and was ashamed.
You said, "It is now twilight. Soon it will
Be night. We are walking slowly home.
It makes no difference about the time of day."
And still I said, "What time is it?
Without sunset, without star rise I cease
To be a man. . . ." Indeed, I was quite absurd,
Lost in a familiar field at twilight
Dizzy from staring at the overcast
Sky of my life and time. I would have
Stopped right there and died had I the strength.
But you without a thought had led me home.

This, then, is the end of speculation—
This certainty about the way you go
Night or day, loved or unloved. The darkened sky
Brings rain, rain yields to starlight,
Stars to the somewhat misty morning.
And clear day, clouding toward the afternoon.

These things like loving have no place in time.
The road runs through them for it can't go round.

LILITH

I was the first made woman. I first wept
Alone in the changed light of evening in a chamber
For love.
I am in the trees when the wind visits them
With altering voices
As the year clothes and unclothes.
Non est Bonum . . . it is not good
To be alone.

I rose with the maples on the evening of the first day
Flaming.
Of all birds I loved the Tanager for his scarlet.
I would have filled all the spaces of his song,
Enfolded him as the orange flame enfolds
The blue of its own cooling heart.
I cannot say what I could not have been:
The plenitude
Meted to his emptiness
The heat of which he dreams in the cold night
And the light
All lost.

Oh Tanager, first and last you are a slave to shadows.

Each tree sings,
The leafed tree with the fullest sound.
I am Lilith, the unmarried,
Whom three strong angels could not haul
Back to Eden.
Let Adam howl like a whipped child
The loss was my loss.
I kneel upon the bank, and take my hair down

Weeping like a woman.
Let exiles and altarless men worship me
As night without stars.
I spread my hair over them.

THE RECLUSE

I

My life is bountiful, although I dwell
Absurdly in it. I am a bird disgracing
This most lovely tree by my poor plumage,
Half grown and badly worn as if unowned.
About me grow such gorgeous blossoms
I have long since called them eyes of God.
On this white tree amid blue flowers of air
I am the only thing improbable.
To my own senses I am all unreal.
This bright world lacing and unlacing
Cannot create me in another sense
But stares out of its luminous blue eyes
Unwondering at my wind-eaten wings.

II

I live beside a stream that does not flow,
And I have grown as still as my profound
And household river. I am as cold as ice
And do not know how light inhabits me
Making my heart a crystal cave, untenanted
By anything but glory. I do well know
That underneath, the sea searches the stream
And claims it, beyond all power to contain
Its meanings, or withhold its tearless well
From ocean's fields, resalted by the rock
The name of which is always Niobe.
And by this sign I know that I shall love
Again, and thereby grow both swift and dark.

III

My house is older than my life and therefore
A continual instruction. Through it
Pours the song of birds as if it were
Not there. I read in Ovid at my table
How men were changed from being men
To something less deceivable, and I
Am changed by solitude until the light
Lives through me and my body is no more
A breeder of shadow. On darker days
The rain inhabits me, dim without sorrow
And chill without love. From my reverie
Woodpeckers wake me with their stony bills
Searching in the rotten walls for food.

IV

In especial I am haunted by Apollo
Who loved Daphne, Daphne who became
A tree. I follow her across the fields
Crying, "I am the god of wisdom offering
Knowledge of the past, and of the present
And of what from the dark source beyond us
Is yet to flow." And I too see her run
With the dark certitude of a natural thing
Knowing this is not love, whatever
Love may be, that at her back cries out
I am a god. Her father was a river
In the vale of Tempe who changed her
Into laurel which is forever green.

V

Something has nested in the chimney
And makes a phantom fire with the roaring
Of its wings, stirring the ashes on the stone
In the act of comforting. I warm myself

At night beside this fire, and listen to
The song in the nest that floats above me like
The sea that lives and does not live in shells.
And who will tell me that I do not pray
(Being unfashionable) with the profoundest right
Of a deserted man to that vague thing
Which has usurped my empty hearth and altar
And is a common bird, and yet unknown
To me except by cries, and by the breath of wings.

VI

Wild iris, the hidden violet, and clover
And a dozen jewels nameless to me
Rise in the rank pasture by the river.
What is more real? And these too evening
Encompasses, and night devours altogether.
Fireflies remember the nightly death
Of flowers, luring the wanderer by the river
Tranced in the fire of memory and the dew
To consecrate himself to quest for those
Ten thousand grails. I am not the knight
Of flowers. I am the beast rather
Seen by Gahereth drinking of the river
From whose belly issued the cry of dogs.

VII

Much has been said in dispraise of memory
And I deny it all. I shall not live
In this place long—the meditation
On the signs and sacred images of desire
Must have an end. This place I shall revisit
On the shrunken stream in autumn coming up
The current in an old tin boat to where
My house untenanted is hid by fainting blooms
Suffered by summer to grow much too long.
And I will greet the god of the place
With temperate rejoicing and call him by the name

I knew when last I loved—and for the dance
The hamadryads will forsake their trees.

VIII

What is this wind which twists all,
Letting nothing be final or blooming,
But all, at once, rooted and wandering?
Is this the hour and the minute of the end,
When the gigantic oak goes straying on the land
And streams withdraw to caverns underground?
Far inland I behold the driven gull
Afloat upon the frothing crests of trees
As on the uninhabitable sea
And I am paralyzed with loneliness
And cannot think except to cry aloud
Holds the wide world any slim and glittering thing
For which my heart's need has not a use and gratefulness.

TALES OF ODYSSEUS

The hallucination of good weather
Can deceive only the young. Others
It maddens, when hair becomes
A crop of crocuses and terrible forsythia
Forks from fragile fingers. To be dead
Is easy and passes into habit,
But to live
Surpasses understanding. The outraged
Senses mourn when flesh unfolds
Like an unreachable conception
Suddenly achieved.

Wrapped in a stinking skin I lay all night
Rehearsing lies, until at dawn he crawled out
Blinking the bright windows of his eyes,
Foul, impotent, sinewy, and old.

I gripped him savagely, and he became
Bright water flowing to the sea;
Then a cold serpent, then a flowering tree.
At last he was a glorious woman. With a knife
I came upon the order of my life.

Conceive a coast shuddering and sublime,
And then a ship utterly cast away,
Its people poured like pollen on the waters—
Think then of rocks gigantic
And the unwatered deserts of the deep they guard,
And marvel how I came ashore
(Being neither wholly god nor wholly man)
My knotted beard wrapped round me like the veil
That Ino gave to one who could not love Calypso
Wholly beautiful . . . . And know
That in the infinite patience of Poseidon
All our impatient imaginings
Are sealed at last,
As by an unimagined consummation.

Thom Gunn

CARNAL KNOWLEDGE

Even in bed I pose: desire may grow
More circumstantial and less circumspect
Each night, but an acute girl would suspect
My thoughts might not be, like my body, bare.
I wonder if you know, or, knowing, care?
You know I know you know I know you know.

I am not what I seem, believe me, so
For the magnanimous pagan I pretend
Substitute a forked creature as your friend.
When darkness lies without a roll or stir
Flaccid, you want a competent poseur,
Whose seeming is the only thing to know.

I prod you, you react. Thus to and fro
We turn, to see ourselves perform the same
Comical act inside the tragic game.
Or is it perhaps simpler: could it be
A mere tear-jerker void of honesty
In which there are no motives left to know?

Lie back. Within a minute I will stow
Your greedy mouth, but will not yet to grips.
'There is a space between the breast and lips.'
Also a space between the thighs and head,
So great, we might as well not be in bed:
For we learn nothing here we did not know.

I hardly hoped for happy thoughts, although
In a most happy sleeping time I dreamt
We did not hold each other in contempt.

Then lifting from my lids night's penny weights
I saw that lack of love contaminates.
You know I know you know I know you know.

Abandon me to stammering, and go;
If you have tears, prepare to cry elsewhere
I know of no emotion we can share.
You romp through protests which I find a bore.
And even now I pose, so now go, for
I know you know.

ON THE MOVE

'Man, you gotta Go.'

The blue jay scuffling in the bushes follows
Some hidden purpose, and the gust of birds
That spurts across the field, the wheeling swallows,
Have nested in the trees and undergrowth.
Seeking their instinct, or their poise, or both,
One moves with an uncertain violence
Under the dust thrown by a baffled sense
Or the dull thunder of approximate words.

On motorcycles, up the road, they come:
Small, black, as flies hanging in heat, the Boys,
Until the distance throws them forth, their hum
Bulges to thunder held by calf and thigh.
In goggles, donned impersonality,
In gleaming jackets trophied with the dust,
They strap in doubt—by hiding it, robust—
And almost hear a meaning in their noise.

Exact conclusion of their hardiness
Has no shape yet, but from known whereabouts
They ride, direction where the tires press.
They scare a flight of birds across the field:

Much that is natural, to the will must yield.
Men manufacture both machine and soul,
And use what they imperfectly control
To dare a future from the taken routes.

It is a part solution, after all.
One is not necessarily discord
On earth; or damned because, half animal,
One lacks direct instinct, because one wakes
Afloat on movement that divides and breaks.
One joins the movement in a valueless world,
Choosing it, till, both hurler and the hurled,
One moves as well, always toward, toward.

A minute holds them, who have come to go:
The self-defined, astride the created will
They burst away; the towns they travel through
Are home for neither bird nor holiness,
For birds and saints complete their purposes.
At worst, one is in motion; and at best,
Reaching no absolute, in which to rest,
One is always nearer by not keeping still.

THE CORRIDOR

A separate place between the thought and felt
The empty hotel corridor was dark.
But here the keyhole shone, a meaning spark.
What fires were latent in it! So he knelt.

Now, at the corridor's much lighter end,
A pierglass hung upon the wall and showed,
As by an easily deciphered code,
Dark, door, and man, hooped by a single band.

He squinted through the keyhole, and within
Surveyed an act of love that frank as air
He was too ugly for, or could not dare,

Or at a crucial moment thought a sin.

Pleasure was simple thus: he mastered it.
If once he acted as participant
He would be mastered, the inhabitant
Of someone else's world, mere shred to fit.

He moved himself to get a better look
And then it was he noticed in the glass
Two strange eyes in a fascinated face
That watched him like a picture in a book.

The instant drove simplicity away—
The scene was altered, it depended on
His kneeling, when he rose they were clean gone
The couple in the keyhole; this would stay.

For if the watcher of the watcher shown
There in the distant glass, should be watched too,
Who can be master, free of others; who
Can look around and say he is alone?

Moreover, who can know that what he sees
Is not distorted, that he is not seen
Distorted by a pierglass, curved and lean?
Those curious eyes, through him, were linked to these—

These lovers altered in the cornea's bend.
What could he do but leave the keyhole, rise,
Holding those eyes as equal in his eyes,
And go, one hand held out, to meet a friend?

BEFORE THE CARNIVAL

A painting by Carl Timner

Look, in the attic, the unentered room,
A naked boy leans on the outspread knees

Of his tall brother lolling in costume,
Tights, vest, and cap, of one who on trapeze
Finds comfort farthest from complacencies.

Behind the little boy and acrobat
Through circling half-light from their downshed musing
Hurries the miser in his double hat;
The dry guitar he holds is still, abusing
All others who play music of their choosing.

And lit by a sudden artificial beam
A smocked pretender with his instrument,
Knowing that he is fragment of a dream,
Smirks none the less with borrowed merriment
And twangs for approbation from the front.

Why should they listen when he sings about
The joy of others that he cannot share?
A sexual gossip with a doll-like pout
He cannot touch the objects of his stare:
A prodigal's reflections swimming there.

The boy, his brother's hand upon his arm,
Sees neither where the lava flow of chance
Overtook habit, for he feels the palm
Of him whose turning muscle's nonchalance
Transforms to clockwork their prepared advance.

He too must pick an instrument at length
For this is painted during carnival:
Shall it be then a simple rung of strength
Or these with many strings where well-trained skill
May touch one while it keeps the others still?

And both must dress for the trooping, but the man
Is yet too active and the boy too young
For cloak or fur of heavy thought. They scan
The pace of silence, by the dancers shown
Robes of bright scarlet, horns that were never blown.

MODES OF PLEASURE

I jump with terror seeing him,
Dredging the bar with that stiff glare
As fiercely as if each whim there
Were passion, whose passion is a whim:

The Fallen Rake, being fallen from
The heights of twenty to middle age,
And helpless to control his rage,
So mean, so few the chances come.

The very beauty of his prime
Was that the triumphs which recurred
In different rooms without a word
Would all be lost some time in time.

Thus he reduced the wild unknown.
And having used each hour of leisure
To learn by rote the modes of pleasure,
The sensual skills as skills alone,

He knows that nothing, not the most
Cunning or sweet, can hold him, still.
Living by habit of the will,
He cannot contemplate the past,

Cannot discriminate, condemned
To the sharpest passion of them all.
Rigid he sits: brave, terrible,
The will awaits its gradual end.

BLACK JACKETS

In the silence that prolongs the span
Rawly of music when the record ends,
   The red-haired boy who drove a van
In weekday overalls but, like his friends,

   Wore cycle boots and jacket here
To suit the Sunday hangout he was in,
   Heard, as he stretched back from his beer,
Leather creak softly round his neck and chin.

   Before him, on a coal-black sleeve
Remote exertion had lined, scratched, and burned
   Insignia that could not revive
The heroic fall or climb where they were earned.

On the other drinkers bent together,
Concocting selves for their impervious kit,
   He saw it as no more than leather
Which, taut across the shoulders grown to it,

   Sent through the dimness of a bar
As sudden and anonymous hints of light
   As those that shipping give, that are
Now flickers in the Bay, now lost in night.

He stretched out like a cat, and rolled
The bitterish taste of beer upon his tongue,
   And listened to a joke being told:
The present was the things he stayed among.

   If it was only loss he wore,
He wore it to assert, with fierce devotion,
   Complicity and nothing more.
He recollected his initiation,

And one especially of the rites.
For on his shoulders they had put tattoos:
   The group's name on the left, The Knights,
And on the right the slogan Born To Lose.

MY SAD CAPTAINS

One by one they appear in
the darkness: a few friends, and
a few with historical
names. How late they start to shine!
but before they fade they stand
perfectly embodied, all

the past lapping them like a
cloak of chaos. They were men
who, I thought, lived only to
renew the wasteful force they
spent with each hot convulsion.
They remind me, distant now.

True, they are not at rest yet,
but now that they are indeed
apart, winnowed from failures,
they withdraw to an orbit
and turn with disinterested
hard energy, like the stars.

SYON HOUSE

a distant sound of water,
dew on blackberry bushes
globing the thorns, glossing
the mauve, slightly whiskered
segments of unripe berries

but there is a mystery: strange
forms push in from outside;
I am oppressed by a sense of columns.
I push back, but their pressure
is continual because
they have no mind or feeling
to vacillate

LEBENSRAUM

Life should be a humane
undertaking. I know. I
undertook it.
                    Yet have found
that in my every move
I prevent someone
from stepping where I step.

So I must run into the open,
alone, to wait on the
untrodden acres of snow
among black trunks, till
the bacillus of despair is
rendered harmless:
isolated and frozen over.

(Poem with a photograph of a very old woman)

Something approaches, about
which she has heard a good deal.
Her deaf ears have caught it, like
a silence in the wainscot
by her head. Her flesh has felt
a chill in her feet, a draught

in her groin. She has watched it
like moonlight on the frayed wood
stealing toward her
floorboard by floorboard. Will it hurt?

Let it come, it is
the terror of full repose,
and so no terror.

(Poem with a photograph of a lined and seamed face)

The memoirs of the body
are inscribed on it: they make
an ambiguous story
because you can read
the lines two ways: as
the ability to resist
annihilation, or as the small
but constant losses endured

but between the lines
life itself! you can read
the plump puckers
                        while
the sentences cross and recross

(Please destroy in
the event of death.)

Anthony Hecht

LA CONDITION BOTANIQUE

    Romans, rheumatic, gouty, came
To bathe in Ischian springs where water steamed,
Puffed and enlarged their bold imperial thoughts, and which
Later Madame Curie declared to be so rich
    In radioactive content as she deemed
      Should win them everlasting fame.

    Scattered throughout their ice and snow
    The Finns have built airtight cabins of log
Where they may lie, limp and entranced by the sedative purr
Of steam pipes, or torment themselves with flails of fir
    To stimulate the blood, and swill down grog,
      Setting the particles aglow.

    Similarly the Turks, but know
    Nothing of the more delicate thin sweat
Of plants, breathing their scented oxygen upon
Brooklyn's botanical gardens, roofed with glass and run
    So to the pleasure of each leafy pet,
      Manured, addressed in Latin, so

    To its thermostatic happiness—
    Spreading its green and innocence to the ground
Where pipes, like Satan masquerading as the snake,
Coil and uncoil their frightful liquid length, and make
    Gurglings of love mixed with a rumbling sound
      Of sharp intestinal distress—

    So to its pleasure, as I said,
    That each particular vegetable may thrive,

Early and late, as in the lot first given Man,
Sans interruption, as when Universal Pan
  Led on the Eternal Spring. The spears of chive,
    The sensitive plant, showing its dread,

    The Mexican flytrap, that can knit
    Its quilled jaws pitilessly, and would hurt
A fly with pleasure, leading Riley's life in bed
Of peat moss and of chemicals, and is thoughtfully fed
    Flies for the entrée, flies for the dessert,
      Fruit flies for fruit, and all of it

      Administered as by a wife—
    Lilith our lady, patroness of plants,
Who sings, *Lullay myn lykyng, myn owyn dere derlyng,*
Madrigals nightly to the spiny stalk in sterling
    Whole notes of admiration and romance—
      This, then, is what is called The Life.

      And we, like disinherited heirs,
    Old Adams, can inspect the void estate
At visiting hours: the unconditional garden spot,
The effortless innocence preserved, for God knows what,
    And think, as we depart by the toll gate:
      No one has lived here these five thousand years.

      Our world is turned on points, is whirled
    On wheels, Tibetan prayer wheels, French verb wheels,
The toothy wheels of progress, the terrible torque
Insisting, and in the sky, even above New York
    Rotate the marvelous four-fangled seals
      Ezekiel saw. The mother-of-pearled

      Home of the bachelor oyster lies
    Fondled in fluent shifts of bile and lime
As sunlight strikes the water, and it is of our world,
And will appear to us sometime where the finger is curled
    Between the frets upon a mandolin,
      Fancy cigar boxes, and eyes

Of ceremonial masks; and all
The places where Kilroy inscribed his name,
For instance, the ladies' rest room in the Gare du Nord,
The iron rump of Buddha, whose hallowed, hollowed core
Admitted tourists once but all the same
Housed a machine gun, and let fall

A killing fire from its eyes
During the war; and Polyphemus hurled
Tremendous rocks that stand today off Sicily's coast
Signed with the famous scrawl of our most traveled ghost;
And all these various things are of our world.
But what's become of Paradise?

Ah, it is lodged in glass, survives
In Brooklyn, like a throwback, out of style,
Like an incomprehensible veteran of the Grand
Army of the Republic in the reviewing stand
Who sees young men in a mud-colored file
March to the summit of their lives,

For glory, for their country, with the flag
Joining divergent stars of North and South
In one blue field of heaven, till they fall in blood
And are returned at last unto their native mud—
The eyes weighed down with stones, the sometimes mouth
Helpless to masticate or gag

Its old inheritance of earth.
In the sweat of thy face shalt thou manage, said the Lord.
And we, old Adams, stare through the glass panes and wince,
Fearing to see the ancestral apple, pear, or quince,
The delicacy of knowledge, the fleshed Word,
The globe of wisdom that was worth

Our lives, or so our parents thought,
And turn away to strengthen our poor breath
And body, keep the flesh rosy with hopeful dreams,

Peach-colored, practical, to decorate the bones, with schemes
 Of life insurance, Ice-Cream-After-Death,
  Hormone injections, against the *mort'*

 Saison, largely to babble praise
 Of Simeon Pyrites, patron saint
Of our Fools' Paradise, whose glittering effigy
Shines in God's normal sunlight till the blind men see
 Visions as permanent as artists paint:
  The body's firm, nothing decays

 Upon the heirloom set of bones
 In their gavotte. Yet we look through the glass
Where green lies ageless under snow-stacked roofs in steam-
Fitted apartments, and reflect how bud and stem
 Are wholly flesh, and the immaculate grass
  Does without buttressing of bones.

 In open field or public bed
 With ultraviolet help, man hopes to learn
The leafy secret, pay his most outstanding debt
To God in the salt and honesty of his sweat,
 And in his streaming face manly to earn
  His daily and all-nourishing bread.

SAMUEL SEWALL

Samuel Sewall, in a world of wigs,
Flouted opinion in his personal hair;
For foppery he gave not any figs,
But in his right and honor took the air.

Thus in his naked style, though well attired,
He went forth in the city, or paid court
To Madam Winthrop, whom he much admired,
Most godly, but yet liberal with the port.

And all the town admired for two full years
His excellent address, his gifts of fruit,
Her gracious ways and delicate white ears,
And held the course of nature absolute.

But yet she bade him suffer a peruke,
"That One be not distinguished from the All";
Delivered of herself this stern rebuke
Framed in the resonant language of St. Paul.

"Madam," he answered her, "I have a Friend
Furnishes me with hair out of His strength,
And He requires only I attend
Unto His charity and to its length."

And all the town was witness to his trust:
On Monday he walked out with the Widow Gibbs,
A pious lady of charm and notable bust,
Whose heart beat tolerably beneath her ribs.

On Saturday he wrote proposing marriage,
And closed, imploring that she be not cruel,
"Your favorable answer will oblige,
Madam, your humble servant, Samuel Sewall."

THE DOVER BITCH

A Criticism of Life

for Andrews Wanning

So there stood Matthew Arnold and this girl
With the cliffs of England crumbling away behind them,
And he said to her, "Try to be true to me,
And I'll do the same for you, for things are bad
All over, etc., etc."
Well now, I knew this girl. It's true she had read
Sophocles in a fairly good translation

And caught that bitter allusion to the sea,
But all the time he was talking she had in mind
The notion of what his whiskers would feel like
On the back of her neck. She told me later on
That after a while she got to looking out
At the lights across the channel, and really felt sad,
Thinking of all the wine and enormous beds
And blandishments in French and the perfumes.
And then she got really angry. To have been brought
All the way down from London, and then be addressed
As sort of a mournful cosmic last resort
Is really tough on a girl, and she was pretty.
Anyway, she watched him pace the room
And finger his watch-chain and seem to sweat a bit,
And then she said one or two unprintable things.
But you mustn't judge her by that. What I mean to say is,
She's really all right. I still see her once in a while
And she always treats me right. We have a drink
And I give her a good time, and perhaps it's a year
Before I see her again, but there she is,
Running to fat, but dependable as they come,
And sometimes I bring her a bottle of *Nuit d'Amour*.

THE ORIGIN OF CENTAURS

for Dimitri Hadzi
But to the girdle do the gods inherit,
Beneath is all the fiend's.—KING LEAR

This mild September mist recalls the soul
        To its own lust;
            On the enchanted lawn
It sees the iron top of the flagpole
        Sublimed away and gone
Into Parnassian regions beyond rust;
And would undo the body to less than dust.

Sundial and juniper have been dispelled
        Into thin air.
    The pale ghost of a leaf
Haunts those uncanny softnesses that felled
      And whitely brought to grief
The trees that only yesterday were there.
The soul recoils into its old despair,

Knowing that though the horizon is at hand,
        Twelve paltry feet
    Refuse to be traversed,
And form themselves before wherever you stand
      As if you were accursed;
While stones drift from the field, and the arbor-seat
Floats toward some *millefleurs* world of summer heat.

Yet from the void where the azalea bush
        Departed hence,
    Sadly the soul must hear
Twitter and cricket where should be all hush,
      And from the belvedere
A muffled grunt survives in evidence
That love must sweat under the weight of sense.

Or so once thought a man in a Greek mist—
        When set aside
    The wine-cup and the wine,
And that deep fissure he alone had kissed,
      All circumscribing line,
Moved to the very edge in one swift stride
And took those shawls of nothing for his bride.

Was it the Goddess herself? Some dense embrace
        Closed like a bath
    Of love about his head;
Perfectly silent and without a face.
      Blindfolded on her bed,
He could see nothing but the aftermath:
Those powerful, clear hoofprints on the path.

THE VOW

In the third month, a sudden flow of blood,
The mirth of tabrets ceaseth, and the joy
Also of the harp. The frail image of God
Lay spilled and formless. Neither girl nor boy,
But yet blood of my blood, nearly my child.
          All that long day
Her pale face turned to the window's mild
          Featureless grey.

And for some nights she whimpered as she dreamed
The dead thing spoke, saying: "Do not recall
Pleasure at my conception. I am redeemed
From pain and sorrow. Mourn rather for all
Who breathlessly issue from the bone gates,
          The gates of horn,
For truly it is best of all the fates
          Not to be born.

"Mother, a child lay gasping for bare breath
On Christmas Eve when Santa Claus had set
Death in the stocking, and the lights of death
Flamed in the tree. O, if you can, forget
You were the child, turn to my father's lips
          Against the time
When his cold hand puts forth its fingertips
          Of jointed lime."

Doctors of Science, what is man that he
Should hope to come to a good end? *The best
Is not to have been born.* And could it be
That Jewish diligence and Irish jest
The consent of flesh and a midwinter storm
          Had reconciled,
Was yet too bold a mixture to inform
          A simple child?

Even as gold is tried, Gentile and Jew.
If that ghost was a girl's, I swear to it:
Your mother shall be far more blessed than you.
And if a boy's, I swear: The flames are lit
That shall refine us; they shall not destroy
        A living hair.
Your younger brothers shall confirm in joy
        This that I swear.

THE MAN WHO MARRIED MAGDALENE

Variation on a Theme by Louis Simpson

> Then said the Lord, dost thou well to be angry?

I have been in this bar
For close to seven days.
The dark girl over there,
For a modest dollar, lays.

And you can get a blow-job
Where other men have pissed
In the little room that's sacred
To the Evangelist—

If you're inclined that way.
For myself, I drink and sleep.
The floor is knotty cedar
But the beer is flat and cheap.

And you can bet your life
I'll be here another seven.
Stranger, here's to my wife,
Who died and went to heaven.

She was a famous beauty,

But *our very breath is loaned.*
The rabbi's voice was fruity,
And since then I've been stoned—

A royal, nonstop bender.
But your money's no good here;
Put it away. Bartender,
Give my friend a beer.

I dreamed the other night
When the sky was full of stars
That I stood outside a gate
And looked in through the bars.

Two angels stood together.
A purple light was shed
From their every metal feather.
And then one of them said,

"It was pretty much the same
For years and years and years,
But since the Christians came
The place is full of queers.

Still, let them have their due.
Things here are far less solemn.
Instead of each beardy Jew
Muttering, 'Shalom, Shalom,'

There's a down-to-earth, informal
Fleshiness to the scene;
It's healthier, more normal,
If you know what I mean

Such as once went to Gehenna
Now dance among the blessed.
But Mary Magdalena
She had it the best."

And he nudged his feathered friend
And gave him a wicked leer,
And I woke up and fought back
The nausea with a beer.

What man shall understand
The Lord's mysterious way?
My tongue is thick with worship
And whiskey, and some day

I will come to in Bellevue
And make psalms unto the Lord.
But verily I tell you,
She hath her reward.

Daryl Hine

THE DOUBLE-GOER

All that I do is clumsy and ill timed.
You move quickly, when it must be done,
To spare yourself or save your victim pain.
And then like the light of the sun you move away
While I come face to face with complex crime
Far from the moving of the mellifluous sea.
All that I do is clumsy and ill timed.
When you perform, my errors pantomimed
Will give an example to the sun
Of flight, and to shadows how to run.
You will in turn discover in my rhyme
Justifications for your simple crime.

Manifold are the disguises of our love.
We change, our transformations turn about,
Our shadowy forms become the doubles for
Affection or hatred. Yet a kind of growth
Is visible, and may be termed the heart,
Confused by the ambiguities of our art.
Manifold are the disguises of our love.
Contradiction of terms is all we have.
To please the self and then the soul
Is difficult and terrible:
Impossible to own a single heart
Lost in the double-dealing of our art.

Two-edged is the double-goer's tongue,
Malice and honey, and the prizes in
His logomachy, what lie near the heart:
Money, honour and success in love.
Harmonious ambiguities in a swarm

Burrow at the fulcrum of his speech.
Two-edged is the double-goer's tongue.
One side says, Right, the other side says, Wrong;
   One, Love is red, the other, Black;
   One, Go on, and one, Turn back.
One hopes for heaven, one for earth, and each
To strike a concord through cross-purposed speech.

So split and halved and twain is every part,
So like two persons severed by a glass
Which darkens the discerning whose is whose
And gives two arms for love and two for hate,
That they cannot discover what they're at
And sometimes think of killing and embrace.
So split and halved and twain is every part,
Double the loins, the fingers, and the heart,
   Confused in object and in aim,
   That they cannot their pleasure name,
But like two doubles in a darkened place
Make one obscure assault and one embrace.

For they were to duality born and bred.
From their childhood the powers of evil were
No less their familiars than the mirror,
Source of a comfortable terror now and then,
And romantic: What good is a fiend unless
I can think and he, my double, act?
Thus we were to duality born and bred.
If these two eyes could turn in the one head,
   Bright orbs by a brighter sphere enclosed,
   Mutually blind and self-opposed,
The right supplying what the left one lacked,
Then I can think, and you, my body, act.

In singleness there is no heart or soul
And solitude is scarcely possible.
The one-sailed ship, tossed on a divided sea
As lightly as cork is tossed, as blindly as
The partners toss on their oceanic bed

And rise and fall, is wrecked and lost away.
In singleness there is no heart or soul;
Thus he sees wrong who sees in halves a whole,
 Who searches heaven but for one,
 And not a double of the sun,
Forgets that, being light as cork, the day
Can rise or fall, is wrecked and lost away.

All that I do is careless and sublime.
You walk head-downwards, now your opened eyes
Take comfort from the beauty of the site.
What if the vision vary in detail?
What are we but sleepers in a cave,
Our dreams the shades of universal doubt?
All that I do is careless and sublime,
You bore with patience to the heart of time;
 Though your resource of art is small
 And my device yields none at all,
Still this two-handed engine will find out
In us the shape and shadow of our doubt.

OSIRIS REMEMBERED

The form of myth is like the life of dream,
Nothing occurs save with significance:
Forgotten baggage in a buried waiting room,
Eurydice condemned by tender glance,
The looks of lovers are not what they seem.
A furious chariot is their ambulance
When they, dispersed, their proper members reassume.

As Theseus abandoned Ariadne
He did not think to see her comforted
On her barren rock amid the amazing sea.
He broke with her as one forbids the dead
And sailed with swift indifference away.

Poor ghost! Her temporary solitude
Was spoiled by Dionysus and by memory.

Once Orpheus had turned his back upon
The saddest and the palest of the shades
And tuned his hymn of praise to the homosexual sun,
He strolled amid the adolescent glades
That moved beside the streams that ceased to run
To music, Dionysus' weakest reeds
Are women. Alas, with them have glades and music gone.

When Theseus destroyed the minotaur
And left the beast to bleed to death within
His maze as complex, still and patterned as the ocean floor,
He dreamt the blood that laced the monster's skin
Had flowed enough, and would be shed no more.
In our veins the vanished creatures win
The fights they lost to us as waves reclaim a shore.

As waves regret the shore they wear away,
As light mourns for the dark it vanquishes,
Orpheus for indistinct Eurydice,
And Theseus, the hero pitiless,
For Ariadne, feel a dreadful pity;
And, moved by this, they shall be consumed by this.
I banished you and you return to punish me.

I hoped this voice eternally was dumb,
I feared these fingers would not move again,
These eyes I thought more vacant than the heart become.
We both had reached the climax of our pain;
Mine stifled yours and halted at its maximum,
I supposed. But I was wrong, for it is plain
You only rested in your absence and waited in that calm.

Tell me if I ought not to rejoice
To see begemmed and thunderous approaching
Through the atmosphere fire flashing in destroys
Among the limb-like kingdoms scarcely touching,

Fatal with the wheels' empurpled noise,
 The furies, my sole chariot of evening,
Yourself remembered and returned. It is a dream. I have no choice.

THE DEVIL'S PICTURE BOOK

Every day it is the same
Inconclusive exercise
Wherein the Old Instructor tries
To teach a patient girl to name
The sentimental verities;
For every substance has a name,
Desire, calculation, shame,
Passion and its properties.

In vain. The pupil will not learn.
She does not see, she says, what life
Sharpness has apart from knife,
Nor why departure spells return.
A leaf to her is just a leaf,
Not a sign that seasons turn,
Though forests *in extremis* burn
And autumn aches beyond relief.

As in a too familiar room
They argue all and every day,
Critical as lovers, they
Dispute what bird and beast assume:
The terror of the verb To Be;
Till, grand in the scholastic gloom,
Propaideutic objects loom
Crude with incredulity.

Why the shabby curtain hung
Across the sky as if congealed,
What landscape was by it concealed,
Which song, as well, the senses sung

Our common education failed
To explain. Thus we were stung
By poetry's demonic tongue:
Where faith was feeling, wit prevailed.

PSYCHE

Precious little is kept in Psyche's whatnot:
Baubles, curious postcards, clues and tangles
Of string—everything you might look for in the
Bulging pockets of thoughtless schoolboys, all but
Hands. There ought to be some connection between
The things she never wants to see again and
Those we lose. Is it quite coincidental?
Childhood's toys cannot speak and suffer later.
Snaps as evidence too are unimportant.
Even that uninventive frantic farewell
That one knew nothing one said now could alter
Turns up legible. Clues belong to someone,
Someone other again involved the love knots.

Still across an unpopulated ballroom
Under musical chandeliers that require
Dusting, consciousness stumbles after lights out,
Where the watery floor lies waxed and frozen
Clumsily without skates she slips and flounders,
Comes, ridiculous, to no false conclusion,
Fidgets, hesitates on the verge of the dance
Toward solitude gaping like a cupboard
In the place of the just about to totter.
All things figure, the world and its abysses,
In a cabinet she pretends to know, which
Others thought to be empty, as if she cared.
Candelabra let fall their notes like snowflakes.

Ask her, what is a whatnot doing in a
Ballroom? Whose is the alibi for those hours

When pretending to sleep beside her husband
She—she too has her pointless secrets; sphinx-like
Psyche complicates what was clear as day this
Morning. Say that we only have three wishes.
One, the easiest, is recourse to silence,
Next, more difficult, is to speak precisely,
Last, implausible, are these riddling hymnals.
Each is only a way of lying and they
Do not matter a fig. So Psyche's answers,
Whether make believe, likely or true, are the
Unique oracle where love is, and why not?

AN ADOLESCENT

Dans le trouble où je suis je ne puis rien pour moi.

Sometimes in front of the deceptive landscape
Someone strolls and pauses, a boy no longer,
Do I recognize the unhandsome stranger
    Once he has spoken?

He who just last year led the schools of children
On the brave new heights and along the river
With the fragile voice that is now forever
    Altered and broken.

On the surface much as he was before the
Dream that brought so many defilements waking
And at which his world became queer and shocking,
    In nothing changed much

Save the way he lives and the dread he lives in
Of the heart that knows and the secret words that
Fearful he must listen to, yes, and look at,
    Sickening must touch,

Flocking thick winged instruments that at bedtime

Force him to behold the vagina's pink shell
Falsely close and falsely reopen, as well
    As the mock penis—

Surely this is not what he prays to nightly?
No more ought he trust his daylight companions,
Uncouth, dull, coarse, idle, delinquent these ones,
    Cupid and Venus.

How he wears his youth's unbecoming belted
Jacket, round his shoulders the armour of age,
Squeezing in his palm a small pen-knife whose edge
    He fingers often.

Now his eyes are full of a tasteless hunger
And his features heavy with resignation;
Set on lip, cheek, brow is the abstract passion
    Love cannot soften,

Staring out from windows where death is pregnant
Under damp curls strung on a rotting forehead
Breathing through his mouth like the fish, cold blooded,
    That in the flood stand

As he floats himself over grief and knowledge;
After childhood's wrongs have been known, forgiven,
Undiscovered still are the ways to live in
    Puberty's wasteland.

Window speaks to window as shade to shadow
Thus, 'Our blinds are drawn and our summer selves dead,
Elsewhere windows twinkle their lights abroad
    Long after sundown.

'Is it all too true what we wished for fondly,
This the very thing that we thought we wanted?
There is no way out, what we prayed is granted,
    Suddenly full grown.

'Shelter have we none, hence our broken shutters,
Tempests blow like kisses through empty spaces,
Weeping North West winds to their salt embraces
    Beg us to open,

'So the days are equal that soon will shorten
To the equal nights and the nights grow longer,
Venus' waiting room and the willing stranger—
    What should we hope then?'

'Open wide your arms wherein darkness lightens,
O your eyes alone may dispel those shadows,
There is no respite from the talking shadows,
    Save in your silence.'

Somewhere winter falls, be it Spring or Autumn,
Through the long, cold stop, through the frozen meanwhile
There is no escape for the young but exile
    Cunning and silence.

John Hollander

THE GREAT BEAR

Even on clear nights, lead the most supple children
Out onto hilltops, and by no means will
They make it out. Neither the gruff round image
From a remembered page nor the uncertain
Finger tracing that image out can manage
To mark the lines of what ought to be there,
Passing through certain bounding stars, until
The whole massive expanse of bear appear
Swinging, across the ecliptic; and, although
The littlest ones say nothing, others respond,
Making us thankful in varying degrees
For what we would have shown them: "There it is!"
"I see it now!" Even "Very like a bear!"
Would make us grateful. Because there is no bear

We blame our memory of the picture: trudging
Up the dark, starlit path, stooping to clutch
An anxious hand, perhaps the outline faded
Then; perhaps could we have retained the thing
In mind ourselves, with it we might have staged
Something convincing. We easily forget
The huge, clear, homely dipper that is such
An event to reckon with, an object set
Across the space the bear should occupy;
But even so, the trouble lies in pointing
At any stars. For one's own finger aims
Always elsewhere: the man beside one seems
Never to get the point. "No! The bright star
Just above my fingertip." The star,

If any, that he sees beyond one's finger

Will never be the intended one. To bring
Another's eye to bear in such a fashion
On any single star seems to require
Something very like a constellation
That both habitually see at night;
Not in the stars themselves, but in among
Their scatter, perhaps, some old familiar sight
Is always there to take a bearing from.
And if the smallest child of all should cry
Out on the wet, black grass because he sees
Nothing but stars, though claiming that there is
Some bear not there that frightens him, we need
Only reflect that we ourselves have need

Of what is fearful (being really nothing)
With which to find our way about the path
That leads back down the hill again, and with
Which to enable the older children standing
By us to follow what we mean by "This
Star," "That one," or "The other one beyond it."
But what of the tiny, scared ones?—Such a bear,
Who needs it? We can still make do with both
The dipper that we always knew was there
And the bright, simple shapes that suddenly
Emerge on certain nights. To understand
The signs that stars compose, we need depend
Only on stars that are entirely there
And the apparent space between them. There

Never need be lines between them, puzzling
Our sense of what is what. What a star does
Is never to surprise us as it covers
The center of its patch of darkness, sparkling
Always, a point in one of many figures.
One solitary star would be quite useless,
A frigid conjecture, true but trifling;
And any single sign is meaningless
If unnecessary. Crab, bull, and ram,
Or frosty, irregular polygons of our own

Devising, or finally the Great Dark Bear
That we can never quite believe is there—
Having the others, any one of them
Can be dispensed with. The bear, of all of them,

Is somehow most like any one, taken
At random, in that we always tend to say
That just because it might be there; because
Some Ancients really traced it out, a broken
And complicated line, webbing bright stars
And fainter ones together; because a bear
Habitually appeared—then even by day
It is for us a thing that should be there.
We should not want to train ourselves to see it.
The world is everything that happens to
Be true. The stars at night seem to suggest
The shapes of what might be. If it were best,
Even, to have it there (such a great bear!
All hung with stars!), there still would be no bear.

DIGGING IT OUT

The icicle finger of death, aimed
At the heart always, melts in the sun
But here at night, now with the porchlight
Spilling over the steps, making snow
More marmoreal than the moon could,
It grows longer and, as it lengthens,
Sharpens. All along the street cars are
Swallowed up in the sarcophagous
Mounds, and digging out had better start
Now, before the impulse to work dies,
Frozen into neither terror nor
Indifference, but a cold longing
For sleep. After a few shovelfuls,
Chopped, pushed, then stuck in a hard white fudge,
Temples pound; the wind scrapes icily

Against the beard of sweat already
Forming underneath most of my face,
And halting for a moment's only
Faltering, never resting. There is
Only freezing here, no real melting
While the thickening silence slows up
The motion of the very smallest
Bits of feeling, even.
                              Getting back
To digging's easier than stopping.
Getting back to the unnerving snow
Seems safer than waiting while the rush
Of blood inside one somewhere, crazed by
The shapes one has allowed his life to
Take, throbs, throbs and threatens. If my heart
Attack itself here in the whitened
Street, would there be bugles and the sound
Of hoofbeats thumping on a hard-packed,
Shiny road of snow? Or is that great
Onset of silences itself a
Great white silence? The crunching of wet
Snow around my knees seems louder, now
That the noises of the fear and what the
Fear is of are louder too, and in
The presence of such sounding depths of
Terror, it is harder than ever
To believe what I have always heard:
That it feels at first like spasms of
Indigestion. The thought, as one shoves
Scrapingly at the snow that always
Seems to happen to things and places
That have been arranged just so, the thought
Of being able to wonder if
Something I'd eaten had disagreed
With me, the while waiting to die, is
Ridiculous. "Was it something I
Felt?" "Something I knew?" "Something I was?"
Seem more the kind of thing that one might
Wonder about, smiling mildly, as

He fell gently no great distance to
The cushioning world that he had dug.
Silently—for to call out something
In this snow would be to bury it.
And heavily, for the weight of self
Is more, perhaps at the end, than can
Be borne.
      No, it is only now, as
I urge the bending blade beneath a
Snow-packed tire for what I know can
Not be the last time that I whimper:
I hate having to own a car; I
Don't want to dig it out of senseless
Snow; I don't want to have to die, snow
Or no snow. As the wind blows up a
Little, fine, white powders are sprinkled
Across the clear windshield. Down along
The street a rustle of no leaves comes
From somewhere. And as I realize
What rest is, pause, and start in on a
New corner, I seem to know that there
Is no such thing as overtaxing,
That digging snow is a rhythm, like
Breathing, loving and waiting for night
To end or, much the same, to begin.

HELICON

Allen said, *I am searching for the true cadence.* Gray
Stony light had flashed over Morningside Drive since noon,
Mixing high in the east with a gray smoky darkness,
Blackened steel trusses of Hell-Gate faintly etched into it,
Gray visionary gleam, revealing the clarity of
Harlem's grid, like a glimpse of a future city below:
When the fat of the land shall have fallen into the dripping pan,
The grill will still be stuck with brown crusts, clinging to
Its bars, and neither in the fire nor out of it.

So is it coming about. But in my unguessing days
Allen said, *They still give you five dollars a pint at St. Luke's,*
No kickback to the interne, either; and I leaned out
Over the parapet and dug my heel in the hard,
Unyielding concrete below, and kicked again, and missed
The feeling of turf with water oozing its way to the top
Or of hard sand, making way for life. And was afraid,
Not for the opening of vessels designed to keep
Their rich dark cargo from the air, but for the kind
Of life that led from this oldest of initiations
Ending in homelessness, despondency and madness,
And for the moment itself when I should enter through
Those dirty-gray stone portals into the hospital
Named for the Greek doctor, abandoning all hope
Of home or of self-help. The heights of Morningside
Sloped downward, to the north, under the iron line
The subway holds to above it, refusing to descend
Under the crashing street. St. John the Divine's gray bulk
Posed, in its parody of history, just in the south.
Dry in the mouth and tired after a night of love
I followed my wild-eyed guide into the darkening door.

Inquiries and directions. Many dim rooms, and the shades
Of patient ghosts in the wards, caught in the privileged
Glimpses that the hurrying visitor always gets;
Turnings; errors; wanderings; while Allen chattered on:
I mean someday to cry out against the cities, but first
I must find the true cadence. We finally emerged
Into a dismal chamber, bare and dusty, where, suddenly,
Sunlight broke over a brown prospect of whirling clouds
And deepening smoke to plummet down, down to the depths
Of the darknesses, where, recessed in a tiny glory of light
A barely-visible man made his way in a boat
Along an amber chasm closing in smoke above him—
Two huge paintings by Thomas Cole opened, like airshaft
Windows, on darkening hearts, there by the blood bank.
We waited then and the dead hospital-white of the cots
Blinded my eyes for a while, and filled my ears with the silence
Of blanketing rushes of blood. Papers and signatures. Waiting;

And then being led by the hand into a corner across
The narrow room from Allen. We both lay down in the whiteness.
The needle struck. There was no pain, and as Allen waved,
I turned to the bubbling fountain, welling down redly beside me
And vanishing into the plasma bottle. My life drained of richness
As the light outside seemed to darken.

                                 Darker and milder the stream
Of blood was than the flashing, foaming spray I remembered
Just then, when, the summer before, with some simple souls who
        knew
Not Allen, I'd helped to fill Columbia's public fountains
With some powdered detergent and concentrated essence of grape,
Having discovered the circulation of water between them
To be a closed system. The sun of an August morning fired
Resplendently overhead; maiden teachers of English
From schools in the south were moving whitely from class to class
When the new, bubbling wine burst from the fountain's summits
Cascading down to the basins. The air was full of grapes
And little birds from afar clustered about their rims,
Not daring to drink, finally, and all was light and wine.
I forgot what we'd felt or said. My trickle of blood had died,
As the light outside seemed to brighten.

                                 Then rest; then five dollars. Then
        Allen
Urged us out onto the street. The wind sang around the corner,
Blowing in from the sound and a siren screeched away
Up Amsterdam Avenue. *Now you have a chocolate malted
And then you're fine,* he said, and the wind blew his hair like feathers,
And we both dissolved into nineteen forty-eight, to be whirled
Away into the wildwood of time, I to leave the city
For the disorganized plain, spectre of the long drink
Taken of me that afternoon. *Turning a guy
On,* said Allen last year to the hip psychiatrists
Down in Atlantic City, *that's the most intimate thing
You can ever do to him.* Perhaps. I have bled since
To many cadences, if not to the constant tune
Of the heart's yielding and now I know how hard it is
To turn the drops that leaky faucets make in unquiet
Nights, the discrete tugs of love in its final scene,

Into a stream, whether thicker or thinner than blood, and I know
That opening up at all is harder than meeting a measure:
With night coming on like a death, a ruby of blood is a treasure.

THE NINTH OF JULY

In 1939 the skylark had nothing to say to me
As the June sunset splashed rose light on the broad sidewalks
And prophesied no war after the end of that August;
Only, midway between playing ball in Manhattan and Poland
I turned in my sleep on Long Island, groped in the dark of July,
And found my pillow at last down at the foot of my bed.
Through the window near her bed, brakes gasped on Avenue B
In 1952; her blonde crotch shadowed and silent
Astonished us both, and the iced gunpowder tea grew warm.
Till the last hollow crust of icecube cracked to its death in the glass.
The tea was hot on the cold hilltop in the moonlight
While a buck thrashed through the gray ghosts of burnt-out trees
And Thomas whispered of the S.S. from inside his sleeping-bag.
Someone else told a tale of the man who was cured of a hurt by the
        bears.
The bathtub drain in the Old Elberon house gucked and snorted
When the shadows of graying maples fell across the lawn:
The brown teddybear was a mild comfort because of his silence,
And I gazed at the porthole ring made by the windowshade
String, hanging silently, seeing a head and shoulders emerge
From the burning *Morro Castle* I'd seen that afternoon.
The rock cried out "I'm burning, too" as the drying heat
Entered its phase of noon over the steep concrete
Walls along Denver's excuse for a river: we read of remote
Bermudas, and gleaming Neal spat out over the parapet.
In the evening in Deal my b.b. rifle shattered a milkbottle
While the rhododendrons burned in the fading light. The tiny
Shot-sized hole in the bathhouse revealed the identical twats
Of the twins from over the hill. From over the hill on the other
Side of the lake a dark cloud turretted over the sunset;
Another lake sank to darkness on the other side of the hill,

Lake echoing lake in diminishing pools of reflection.
A trumpet blew Taps. While the drummer's foot boomed on the
    grandstand
The furriers' wives by the pool seemed to ignore the accordion
Playing "Long Ago and Far Away." None of the alewives
Rose to our nightcrawlers, wiggling on the other side of the mirror.
She was furrier under the darkness of all the blanketing heat
Than I'd thought to find her, and the bathroom mirror flashed
White with the gleam of a car on seventy-second street.
We lay there just having died; the two of us, vision and flesh,
Contraction and dream, came apart, while the fan on the windowsill
Blew a thin breeze of self between maker and muse, dividing
Fusing of firework, love's old explosion and outburst of voice.

This is the time most real: for unreeling time there are no
Moments, there are no points, but only the lines of memory
Streaking across the black film of the mind's night.
But here in the darkness between two great explosions of light,
Midway between the fourth of July and the fourteenth,
Suspended somewhere in summer between the ceremonies
Remembered from childhood and the historical conflagrations
Imagined in sad, learned youth—somewhere there always hangs
The American moment.
                      Burning, restless, between the deed
And the dream is the life remembered: the sparks of Concord were
    mine
As I lit a cherry-bomb once in a glow of myth
And hurled it over the hedge. The complexities of the Terror
Were mine as my poring eyes got burned in the fury of Europe
Discovered in nineteen forty-two. On the ninth of July
I have been most alive; world and I, in making each other
As always, make fewer mistakes.
                      The gibbous, historical moon
Records our nights with an eye neither narrowed against the
    brightness
Of nature, nor widened with awe at the clouds of the life of the
    mind.
Crescent and full, knowledge and touch commingled here
On this dark bed, window flung wide to the cry of the city night.

We lie still, making the poem of the world that emerges from
     shadows.

Doing and then having done is having ruled and commanded
A world, a self, a poem, a heartbeat in the moonlight.

To imagine a language means to imagine a form of life.

UNDER CANCER

On the Memorial building's
Terrace the sun has been buzzing
Unbearably, all the while
The white baking happens
To the shadow of the table's
White-painted iron. It darkens,
Meaning that the sun is stronger,
That I am invisibly darkening
Too, the while I whiten.
And only after the stretching
And getting up, still sweating,
My shirt striped like an awning
Drawn on over airlessness;
After the cool shades
(As if of a long arcade
Where footsteps echo gravely)
Have devoured the light;
Only after the cold of
Plunge and shower, the pale
Scent of deodorant stick
Smelling like gin and limes,
And another stripy shirt
Can come, homing in at last,
The buzzing of having been burnt.
Only then, intimations
Of tossing, hot in the dark
Night, where all the long while

Silently, along edges,
There is flaking away.

In this short while of light
My shadow darkens without
Lengthening ever, ever.

THE NIGHT MIRROR

What it showed was always the same—
A vertical panel with him in it,
Being a horrible bit of movement
At the edge of knowledge, overhanging
The canyons of nightmare. And when the last
Glimpse was enough—his grandmother,
Say, with a blood-red face, rising
From her Windsor chair in the warm lamplight
To tell him something—he would scramble up,
Waiting to hear himself shrieking, and gain
The ledge of the world, his bed, lit by
The pale rectangle of window, eclipsed
By a dark shape, but a shape that moved
And saw and knew and mistook its reflection
In the tall panel on the closet door
For itself. The silver corona of moonlight
That gloried his glimpsed head was enough
To send him back into silences, choosing
Fear in those chasms below, to reject
Freedom of wakeful seeing, believing
And feeling, for peace, and the bondage to horrors
Welling up only from deep within
That dark planet head, spinning beyond
The rim of the night mirror's range, huge
And cold, on the pillow's dark side.

A. D. Hope

THE GATEWAY

Now the heart sings with all its thousand voices
To hear this city of cells, my body, sing.
The tree through the stiff clay at long last forces
Its thin strong roots and taps the secret spring.

And the sweet waters without intermission
Climb to the tips of its green tenement;
The breasts have borne the grace of their possession,
The lips have felt the pressure of content.

Here I come home: in this expected country
They know my name and speak it with delight.
I am the dream and you my gates of entry,
The means by which I waken into light.

AUSTRALIA

A Nation of trees, drab green and desolate grey
In the field uniform of modern wars,
Darkens her hills, those endless, outstretched paws
Of Sphinx demolished or stone lion worn away.

They call her a young country, but they lie:
She is the last of lands, the emptiest,
A woman beyond her change of life, a breast
Still tender but within the womb is dry.

Without songs, architecture, history:
The emotions and superstitions of younger lands,

Her rivers of water drown among inland sands,
The river of her immense stupidity

Floods her monotonous tribes from Cairns to Perth.
In them at last the ultimate men arrive
Whose boast is not: "we live" but "we survive",
A type who will inhabit the dying earth.

And her five cities, like five teeming sores,
Each drains her: a vast parasite robber-state
Where second-hand Europeans pullulate
Timidly on the edge of alien shores.

Yet there are some like me turn gladly home
From the lush jungle of modern thought, to find
The Arabian desert of the human mind,
Hoping, if still from the deserts the prophets come,

Such savage and scarlet as no green hills dare
Springs in that waste, some spirit which escapes
The learned doubt, the chatter of cultured apes
Which is called civilization over there.

THE ELEGY

Variations on a theme of the Seventeenth Century

Madam, no more! The time has come to eat.
The spirit of man is nourished, too, with meat.
Those heroes and the warriors of old—
Feasting between their battles made them bold.
When Venus in the west hung out her lamp,
The rattling sons of Mars marched home to camp;
And while around the fires their wounds were dressed,
And tale was matched with tale, and jest with jest,
Flagons of wine and oxen roasted whole

Refreshed their bodies and restored the soul.

Come, leave the bed; put on your dress; efface
Awhile this dazzling armoury of grace!
Flushed and rejoicing from the well-fought fight
Now day lies panting in the arms of night;
The first dews tremble on the darkening field;
Put up your naked weapons, the bright shield
Of triumph glinting to the early stars;
Call our troops home with trumpets from their wars;
And, as wise generals, let them rest and dine
And celebrate our truce with meat and wine.
See, the meek table on our service waits;
The devil in crystal winks beside our plates;
These veterans of love's war we shall repay
And crown with feasts the glories of the day.

Think no disgrace, if now they play a part
Less worthy of the soldiers of the heart.
Though these we led were granted, even as we,
Their moment's draught of immortality,
We do but snatch our instant on the height
And in the valleys still live out the night.
Yet they surrender nothing which is theirs.
Nature is frugal in her ministers;
Each to some humbler office must return,
And so must we. Then grudge it not, but learn
In this the noble irony of kind:
These fierce, quick hands that rove and clasp must find
Other employment now with knife and fork;
Our mouths that groaned with joy, now eat and talk;
These chief commanders, too, without debate,
Sink to the lowliest service of the state.
Only our eyes observe no armistice;
Sparkling with love's perpetual surprise,
Their bright vedettes keep watch from hill to hill
And, when they meet, renew the combat still.
And yet to view you would I linger on:

This is the rarest moment, soonest gone.
While now the marching stars invest the sky
And the wide lands beneath surrendered lie,
Their streams and forests, parks and fields and farms,
Like this rich empire tranquil in my arms,
Seem lovelier in the last withdrawing light
And, as they vanish, most enchant the sight.
Still let me watch those countries as they fade
And all their lucid contours sink in shade;
The mounting thighs, the line of flank and breast,
Yet harbour a clear splendour from the west;
Though twilight draws into its shadowy reign
This breathing valley and that glimmering plain,
Still let my warrior heart with fresh delight
Rove and reflect: "Here, here began the fight;
Between those gentle hills I paused to rest,
And on this vale the kiss of triumph pressed;
There, full encircled by the frantic foe,
I rode between the lilies and the snow;
And, in this copse that parts the dark and shine,
Plundered the treasures of the hidden mine;
Down those long slopes in slow retreat I drew;
And here renewed the charge; and here, anew
Met stroke with stroke and touched, at the last breath,
The unimagined ecstasy of death."

Full darkness! Time enough the lamps were lit.
Let us to dinner, Madam; wine and wit
Must have their hour, even as love and war,
And what's to come revives what went before.
Come now, for see the Captain of my lust,
He had so stoutly fought and stiffly thrust,
Fallen, diminished on the field he lies;
Cover his face, he dreams in paradise.
We, while he sleeps, shall dine; and, when that's done,
Drink to his resurrection later on.

IMPERIAL ADAM

Imperial Adam, naked in the dew,
Felt his brown flanks and found the rib was gone.
Puzzled he turned and saw where, two and two,
The mighty spoor of Jahweh marked the lawn.

Then he remembered through mysterious sleep
The surgeon fingers probing at the bone,
The voice so far away, so rich and deep:
"It is not good for him to live alone."

Turning once more he found Man's counterpart
In tender parody breathing at his side.
He knew her at first sight, he knew by heart
Her allegory of sense unsatisfied.

The pawpaw drooped its golden breasts above
Less generous than the honey of her flesh;
The innocent sunlight showed the place of love;
The dew on its dark hairs winked crisp and fresh.

This plump gourd severed from his virile root,
She promised on the turf of Paradise
Delicious pulp of the forbidden fruit;
Sly as the snake she loosed her sinuous thighs,

And waking, smiled up at him from the grass;
Her breasts rose softly and he heard her sigh—
From all the beasts whose pleasant task it was
In Eden to increase and multiply

Adam had learned the jolly deed of kind:
He took her in his arms and there and then,
Like the clean beasts, embracing from behind,
Began in joy to found the breed of men.

Then from the spurt of seed within her broke
Her terrible and triumphant female cry,
Split upward by the sexual lightning stroke.
It was the beasts now who stood watching by:

The gravid elephant, the calving hind,
The breeding bitch, the she-ape big with young
Were the first gentle midwives of mankind;
The teeming lioness rasped her with her tongue;

The proud vicuña nuzzled her as she slept
Lax on the grass; and Adam watching too
Saw how her dumb breasts at their ripening wept,
The great pod of her belly swelled and grew,

And saw its water break, and saw, in fear,
Its quaking muscles in the act of birth,
Between her legs a pigmy face appear,
And the first murderer lay upon the earth.

THE DOUBLE LOOKING GLASS

See how she strips her lily for the sun:
The silk shrieks upward from her wading feet;
Down through the pool her wavering echoes run;
Candour with candour, shade and substance meet.

From where a wet meniscus rings the shin
The crisp air shivers up her glowing thighs,
Swells round a noble haunch and whispers in
The dimple of her belly. . . . Surely eyes

Lurk in the laurels, where each leafy nest
Darts its quick bird-glance through the shifting screen.
. . . . Yawn of the oxter, lift of liquid breast
Splinter their white shafts through our envious green

Where thuds this rage of double double hearts.
. . . . My foolish fear refracts a foolish dream.
Here all things have imagined counterparts:
A dragon-fly dim-darting in the stream

Follows and watches with enormous eyes
His blue narcissus glitter in the air.
The flesh reverberates its own surprise
And startles at the act which makes it bare.

Laced with quick air and vibrant to the light,
Now my whole animal breathes and knows its place
In the great web of being, and its right;
The mind learns ease again, the heart finds grace.

I am as all things living. Man alone
Cowers from his world in clothes and cannot guess
How earth and water, branch and beast and stone
Speak to the naked in their nakedness.

. . . . A silver rising of her arms, that share
Their pure and slender crescent with the pool
Plunders the braided treasure of her hair.
Loosed from their coils uncrowning falls the full

Cascade of tresses whispering down her flanks,
And idly now she wades a step, and stays
To watch the ripples widen to the banks
And lapse in mossy coves and rushy bays.

Look with what bliss of motion now she turns
And seats herself upon a sunny ledge,
Leans back, and drowsing dazzles, basking burns.
Susannah! . . . . what hiss, what rustle in the sedge;

What fierce susurrus shifts from bush to bush?
. . . . Susannah! Susannah, Susannah! . . . . Foolish heart,
It was your own pulse lisping in a hush
So deep, I hear the water-beetle dart

And trace from bank to bank his skein of light,
So still the sibilance of a breaking bud
Speaks to the sense; the hairy bee in flight
Booms a brute chord of danger in my blood.

What danger though? The garden wall is high
And bolted and secure the garden door;
The bee, bold ravisher, will pass me by
And does not seek my honey for his store;

The speckled hawk in heaven, wheeling slow
Searches the tufts of grass for other prey;
Safe in their sunny banks the lilies grow,
Secure from rough hands for another day.

Alert and brisk, even the hurrying ant
Courses these breathing ranges unafraid.
The fig-tree, leaning with its leaves aslant,
Touches me with broad hands of harmless shade.

And if the urgent pulses of the sun
Quicken my own with a voluptuous heat,
They warm me only as they warm the stone
Or the thin liquid paddling round my feet.

My garden holds me like its private dream,
A secret pleasure, guarded and apart.
Now as I lean above the pool I seem
The image of my image in its heart.

A mirror for man's images of love
The nakedness of woman is a pool
In which her own desires mount and move,
Alien, solitary, purposeful

Yet in this close were every leaf an eye,
In those green limbs the sap would mount as slow.
One with their life beneath an open sky,
I melt into the trance of time, I flow

Into the languid current of the day
. . . . The sunlight sliding on a breathing flank
Fades and returns again in tranquil play;
Her eyelids close; she sleeps upon the bank.

Now, now to wreak upon her Promised Land
The vengeance of the dry branch on the bud.
Who shall be first upon her? Who shall stand
To watch the dragon sink its fangs in blood?

Her ripeness taunts the ignominy of age;
Seethes in old loins with hate and lust alike.
Now in the plenitude of shame and rage
The rod of chastisement is reared to strike.

And now to take her drowsing; now to fall
With wild-fire on the cities of the plain;
Susannah! . . . . Yet once more that hoarse faint call,
That rustle from the thicket comes again?

Ah, no! Some menace from the edge of sleep
Imposes its illusion on my ear.
Relax, return, Susannah; Let the deep
Warm tide of noonday bear you; do not fear,

But float once more on that delicious stream.
Suppose some lover watches from the grove;
Suppose, only suppose, those glints, the gleam
Of eyes; the eyes of a young man in love.

Shall I prolong this fancy, now the sense
Impels, the hour invites? Shall I not own
Such thoughts as women find to recompense
Their hidden lives when secret and alone?

Surprise the stranger in the heart, some strong
Young lion of the rocks who found his path
By night, and now he crouches all day long
Beside the pool to see me at my bath.

He would be there, a melancholy shade
Caught in the ambush of his reckless joy,
Afraid to stir for fear I call, afraid
In one unguarded moment to destroy

At once the lover and the thing he loves.
Who should he be? I cannot guess; but such
As desperate hope or lonelier passion moves
To tempt his fate so far, to dare so much;

Who having seen me only by the way,
Or having spoken with me once by chance,
Fills all his nights with longing, and the day
With schemes whose triumph is a casual glance.

Possessed by what he never can possess,
He forms his wild design and ventures all
Only to see me in my nakedness
And lurk and tremble by the garden wall.

He lives but in my dream, I need repel
No dream for I may end it when I please;
And I may dream myself in love as well
As dream my lover in the summer trees,

Suppose myself desired, suppose desire,
Summon that wild enchantment of the mind,
Kindle my fire at his imagined fire,
Pity his love and call him and be kind.

Now think he comes, and I shall lie as still
As limpid waters that reflect their sun,
And let him lie between my breasts and fill
My loins with thunder till the dream be done.

The kisses of my mouth are his; he lies
And feeds among the lilies; his brown knees
Divide the white embraces of my thighs.
Wake not my love nor stir him till he please,

For now his craft has passed the straits and now
Into my shoreless sea he drives alone.
Islands of spice await his happy prow
And fabulous deeps support and bear him on.

He rides the mounting surge, he feels the wide
Horizon draw him onward mile by mile;
The reeling sky, the dark rejoicing tide
Lead him at last to this mysterious isle.

In ancient woods that murmur with the sea,
He finds once more the garden and the pool.
And there a man who is and is not he
Basks on the sunny margin in the full

Noon of another and a timeless sky,
And dreams but never hopes to have his love;
And there the woman who is also I
Watches him from the hollow of the grove;

Till naked from the leaves she steals and bends
Above his sleep and wakes him with her breast
And now the vision begins, the voyage ends,
And the great phoenix blazes in his nest.

. . . . Ah, God of Israel, even though alone,
We take her with a lover, in the flush
Of her desires. SUSANNAH! . . . . I am undone!
What beards, what bald heads burst now from the bush!

THE LINGAM AND THE YONI

The Lingam and the Yoni
Are walking hand in glove,
O are you listening, honey?
I hear my honey-love.

The He and She our movers
What is it they discuss?
Is it the talk of Lovers?
And do they speak of us?

I hear their high palaver—
O tell me what they say!
The talk goes on for ever
So deep in love are they;

So deep in thought, debating
The suburb and the street;
Time-payment calculating
Upon the bedroom suite.

But ours is long division
By love's arithmetic,
Until they make provision
To buy a box of brick,

A box that makes her prisoner,
That he must slave to win
To do the Lingam honour,
To keep the Yoni in.

The mortgage on tomorrow?
The haemorrhage of rent?
Against the heart they borrow
At five or six per cent.

The heart has bought fulfilment
Which yet their mouths defer
Until the last instalment
Upon the furniture.

No Lingam for her money
Can make up youth's arrears:
His layby on the Yoni
Will not be paid in years.

And they, who keep this tally,
They count what they destroy;
While, in its secret valley
Withers the herb of joy.

Richard Howard

ADDRESS UNKNOWN

Hurrying the tired heart
From worry tonight homeward
And fast over hills beyond
Here to somewhere eagerly
Else, love, run, run to your rest.

Standing stock-still I marvel
How much you so resemble
The imp of promises I
At best improvidently
Took you for in old weather . . .

Comes the broken time, labels
Even of a light travel
Lie as of a dark. Look how
The burning countries oh far
Away grow black down again.

RUMORS OF REAL ESTATE

He speaks of a white room showing
Barest at night, shadowed only
By the lamp under which his cat,
White as well, warms in a brightness
Of refusals. Of course there are
Imperfections, but until now
He has been able to shut them
Up or away, into darkness
Behind the blank of his white doors.

Naturally we all suspect

Some other sort of chamber where
He works his living out, warden
Of an implicating space: not
Only purple with unexplained
Obscurities, but gathering
All time in images of dim
Insistences. A various
Room, and full of forms, reflections.

But the truth is down a long hall
And in another place. Here are
Cruel colors, terrible cold
And a burning quite as extreme.
On the changeable bed someone
Else is lying and lying quite
Miserably. Now, following
Trials of temperature, come
Tests on teeth, examination

Nail by broken nail, and nightly
Obligation to employ each
Bright instrument that hangs upon
Its hook. This is a right surround,
Binding blur to brutality—
The genuine decor. How pat
Our word *apartment* falls in here,
For this is the life he divides
From the others, a death apart.

FURTHER INSTRUCTIONS TO
THE ARCHITECT

Now about the attic: please allow
    For easy access to the roof
So Lois can sun-bathe out there.
    Fall, did you say? Remember all
    The servants' bedrooms must include
A dream book in the dresser, and there was

Always a gate across the stairs:
Our pantry sibyl walked in her sleep,
    Read tea-leaves, knew what "horses" meant.

Make sure the smell of apple peel
    Lingers in the master-bedroom,
Keep lewd prints for the *Decameron*
Locked in the library, and repair
    The stained glass over the landing:
If the Lorelei's locks are still there
The amber can always be replaced.
    I hear one ilex has fallen
Across the pond. Better plant rushes
    So the frogs will come back, evenings,
And sing their songs; restore the *allée*
Of Lombardy poplars where the doves
    Nested: we need all our mourners.

See that the four black junipers
Don't overgrow the lawn: after dark
    The silver grass is luminous
Around them. There should be a wheezing
French bulldog on my grandmother's lap,
    Of course, and the sound of grape seeds
    Being flicked onto the porch floor
Where Ernestine is reading. Even
The corridor back to whatever
    Surprise you have in store must be
Merely the one between the (witch's)
    Kitchen and the dim hall closet
Where velveteen hangers may have turned
By now to something else unlikely.

You can't help getting it right if you
    Listen to me. Recognition
Is not to be suppressed. Why the whole
Place seems just the way it was, I tell you
    I was there last night: in dreams
We are always under house arrest.

Ted Hughes

THE THOUGHT-FOX

I imagine the midnight moment's forest:
Something else is alive
Beside the clock's loneliness
And this blank page where my fingers move.

Through the window I see no star:
Something more near
Though deeper within darkness
Is entering the loneliness:

Cold, delicately as the dark snow,
A fox's nose touches twig, leaf;
Two eyes serve a movement, that now
And again now, and now, and now

Sets neat prints into the snow
Between trees, and warily a lame
Shadow lags by stump and in hollow
Of a body that is bold to come

Across clearings, an eye,
A widening deepening greenness,
Brilliantly, concentratedly,
Coming about its own business

Till, with a sudden sharp hot stink of fox
It enters the dark hole of the head.
The window is starless still; the clock ticks,
The page is printed.

HAWK ROOSTING

I sit in the top of the wood, my eyes closed.
Inaction, no falsifying dream
Between my hooked head and hooked feet:
Or in sleep rehearse perfect kills and eat.

The convenience of the high trees!
The air's buoyancy and the sun's ray
Are of advantage to me;
And the earth's face upward for my inspection.

My feet are locked upon the rough bark.
It took the whole of Creation
To produce my foot, my each feather:
Now I hold Creation in my foot

Or fly up, and revolve it all slowly—
I kill where I please because it is all mine.
There is no sophistry in my body:
My manners are tearing off heads—

The allotment of death.
For the one path of my flight is direct
Through the bones of the living.
No arguments assert my right:

The sun is behind me.
Nothing has changed since I began.
My eye has permitted no change.
I am going to keep things like this.

A DREAM OF HORSES

We were born grooms, in stable-straw we sleep still,
All our wealth horse-dung and the combings of horses,
And all we can talk about is what horses ail.

Out of the night that gulfed beyond the palace-gate
There shook hooves and hooves and hooves of horses:
Our horses battered their stalls; their eyes jerked white.

And we ran out, mice in our pockets and straw in our hair,
Into darkness that was avalanching to horses
And a quake of hooves. Our lantern's little orange flare

Made a round mask of our each sleep-dazed face,
Bodiless, or else bodied by horses
That whinnied and bit and cannoned the world from its place.

The tall palace was so white, the moon was so round,
Everything else this plunging of horses
To the rim of our eyes that strove for the shapes of the sound.

We crouched at our lantern, our bodies drank the din,
And we longed for a death trampled by such horses
As every grain of the earth had hooves and mane.

We must have fallen like drunkards into a dream
Of listening, lulled by the thunder of the horses.
We awoke stiff; broad day had come.

Out through the gate the unprinted desert stretched
To stone and scorpion; our stable-horses
Lay in their straw, in a hag-sweat, listless and wretched.

Now let us, tied, be quartered by these poor horses,
If but doomsday's flames be great horses,
The forever itself a circling of the hooves of horses.

PIBROCH

The sea cries with its meaningless voice,
Treating alike its dead and its living,
Probably bored with the appearance of heaven
After so many millions of nights without sleep,
Without purpose, without self-deception.

Stone likewise. Stone is imprisoned
Like nothing in the Universe.
Created for black sleep. Or growing
Conscious of the sun's red spot occasionally,
Then dreaming it is the foetus of God.

Over the stone rushes the wind,
Able to mingle with nothing,
Like the hearing of the blind stone itself.
Or turns, as if the stone's mind came feeling
A fantasy of directions.

Drinking the sea and eating the rock
A tree struggles to make leaves—
An old woman fallen from space
Unprepared for these conditions.
She hangs on, because her mind's gone completely.

Minute after minute, aeon after aeon,
Nothing lets up or develops.
And this is neither a bad variant nor a tryout.
This is where the staring angels go through.
This is where all the stars bow down.

Kenneth Koch

LUNCH

The lanternslides grinding out B-flat minor
Chords to the ears of the deaf youngster who sprays in Hicksville
The sides of a car with the dream-splitting paint
Of pianos (he dreamt of one day cutting the Conservatory
In two with his talent), these lanternslides, I say,
They are— The old woman hesitated. A lifesaver was shoved down
      her throat; then she continued:
They are some very good lanternslides in that bunch. Then she
      fainted
And we revived her with flowers. She smiled sleepily at the sun.
He is my own boy, she said, with her glass hand falling through the
      sparkling red America of lunch.

That old boilermaker she has in her back yard,
Olaf said, used to be her sweetheart years back.
One day, though, a train passed, and pressed her hard,
And she deserted life and love for liberty.
We carried Olaf softly into the back yard
And laid him down with his head under the steamroller.
Then Jill took the wheel and I tinkered with the engine,
Till we rolled him under, rolled him under the earth.
When people ask us what's in our back yard
Now, we don't like to tell them, Jill says, laying her silver bandannaed
      head on my greened bronze shoulder.
Then we both dazzle ourselves with the red whiteness of lunch.

That old woman named Tessie Runn
Had a tramp boyfriend who toasted a bun.
They went to Florida, but Maxine Schweitzer was hard of
Hearing and the day afterwards the judge adjourned the trial.
When it finally came for judgment to come up

169

Of delicious courtyards near the Pantheon,
At last we had to let them speak, the children whom flowers had made
    statues
For the rivers of water which came from their funnel;
And we stood there in the middle of existence
Dazzled by the white paraffin of lunch.

Music in Paris and water coming out from the flannel
Of the purist person galloping down the Madeleine
Toward a certain wafer. Hey! just a minute! the sunlight is being
    rifled
By the green architecture of the flowers. But the boulevard turned a
    big blue deaf ear
Of cinema placards to the detonated traveler. He had forgotten the
    blue defilade of lunch!

Genoa! a stone's throw from Acapulco
If an engine were built strong enough,
And down where the hulls and scungilli,
Glisteningly unconscious, agree,
I throw a game of shoes with Horace Sturnbul
And forget to eat lunch.

O launch, lunch, you dazzling hoary tunnel
To paradise!
Do you see that snowman tackled over there
By summer and the sea? A boardwalk went to Istanbul
And back under his left eye. We saw the Moslems praying
In Rhodes. One had a red fez, another had a black cap.
And in the extended heat of afternoon,
As an ice-cold gradual sweat covered my whole body,
I realized, and the carpet swam like a red world at my feet
In which nothing was green, and the Moslems went on praying,
That we had missed lunch, and a perpetual torrent roared into the sea
Of my understanding. An old woman gave us bread and rolls on the
    street.

The dancing wagon has come! here is the dancing wagon!
Come up and get lessons—here is lemonade and grammar!

Here is drugstore and cowboy—all that is America—plus sex, per-
      fumes, and shimmers—all the Old World;
Come and get it—and here is your reading matter
For twenty-nine centuries, and here finally is lunch—
To be served in the green defilade under the roaring tower
Where Portugal meets Spain inside a flowered madeleine.

My ginger dress has nothing on, but yours
Has on a picture of Queen Anne Boleyn
Surrounded by her courtiers eating lunch
And on the back a one of Henry the Eighth
Summoning all his courtiers in for lunch.

And the lunchboat has arrived
From Spain.
Everyone getting sick is on it;
The bold people and the sadists are on it;
I am glad I am not on it,
I am having a big claw of garlic for lunch—
But it plucks me up in the air,
And there, above the ship, on a cloud
I see the angels eating lunch.
One has a beard, another a moustache,
And one has some mustard smeared on his ears.
A couple of them ask me if I want to go to Honolulu,
And I accept—it's all right—
Another time zone: we'll be able to have lunch.
They are very beautiful and transparent,
My two traveling companions,
And they will go very well with Hawaii
I realize as we land there,
That dazzling red whiteness—it is our desire . . .
For whom? The angels of lunch.

Oh I sat over a glass of red wine
And you came out dressed in a paper cup.
An ant-fly was eating hay-mire in the chair-rafters
And large white birds flew in and dropped edible animals to the
      ground.

If they had been gulls it would have been garbage
Or fish. We have to be fair to the animal kingdom,
But if I do not wish to be fair, if I wish to eat lunch
Undisturbed—? The light of day shines down. The world continues.

We stood in the little hutment in Biarritz
Waiting for lunch, and your hand clasped mine
And I felt it was sweaty;
And then lunch was served,
Like the bouquet of an enchantress.
Oh the green whites and red yellows
And purple whites of lunch!

The bachelor eats his lunch,
The married man eats his lunch,
And old Uncle Joris belches
The seascape in which a child appears
Eating a watermelon and holding a straw hat.
He moves his lips as if to speak
But only sea air emanates from this childish beak.
It is the moment of sorrows,
And in the shores of history,
Which stretch in both directions, there are no happy tomorrows.
But Uncle Joris holds his apple up and begins to speak
To the child. Red waves fan my universe with the green macaw of
        lunch.

This street is deserted;
I think my eyes are empty;
Let us leave
Quickly.
Day bangs on the door and is gone.

Then they picked him up and carried him away from that company.
When he awoke he was in the fire department, and sleepy but not
        tired.
They gave him a hoseful of blue Spain to eat for lunch,
And Portugal was waiting for him at the door, like a rainstorm of
        evening raspberries.

It is time to give lunch to my throat and not my chest.
What? either the sting ray has eaten my lunch
Or else—and she searches the sky for something else;
But I am far away, seeming blue-eyed, empirical . . .
Let us give lunch to the lunch—
But how shall we do it?
The headwaiters expand and confer;
Will little pieces of cardboard box do it?
And what about silver and gold pellets?
The headwaiters expand and confer:
And what if the lunch should refuse to eat anything at all?
Why then we'd say be damned to it,
And the red doorway would open on a green railway
And the lunch would be put in a blue car
And it would go away to Whippoorwill Valley
Where it would meet and marry Samuel Dogfoot, and bring forth seven
    offspring,
All of whom would be half human, half lunch;
And when we saw them, sometimes, in the gloaming,
We would take off our mining hats and whistle Tweet twee-oo,
With watering mouths staring at the girls in pink organdy frocks,
Not realizing they really were half edible,
And we would die still without knowing it;
So to prevent anything happening that terrible
Let's give everybody we see and like a good hard bite right now,
To see what they are, because it's time for lunch!

TAKING A WALK WITH YOU

My misunderstandings: for years I thought "muso bello" meant
    "Bell Muse," I thought it was a kind of
Extra reward on the slotmachine of my shyness in the snow when
February was only a bouncing ball before the Hospital of the Two
    Sister of the Last
Hamburger Before I Go to Sleep. I thought Axel's Castle was a
    garage;

And I had beautiful dreams about it, too—sensual, mysterious
    mechanisms; horns honking, wheels turning . . .
My misunderstandings were:
1)   thinking Pinocchio could really change from a puppet into a real
    boy, and back again!
2)   thinking it depended on whether he was good or bad!
3)   identifying him with myself!
4)   and therefore every time I was bad being afraid I would turn
    into wood . . .
5)   I misunderstood childhood. I usually liked the age I was.
    However, now I regard twenty-nine as an optimum age (for me).
6)   I disliked Shelley between twenty and twenty-five.
All of these things I suppose are understandable, but
When you were wearing your bodice I did not understand that you
    had nothing on beneath it;
When my father turned the corner I misunderstood the light very
    much
On Fifty-fifth Street; and I misunderstood (like an old Chinese
    restaurant) what he was doing there.
I misunderstand generally Oklahoma and Arkansas, though I think I
    understand New Mexico;
I understand the Painted Desert, cowboy hats, and vast spaces; I do
Not understand hillbilly life—I am sure I misunderstand it.
I did not understand that you had nothing on beneath your bodice
Nor, had I understood this, would I have understood what it meant;
    even now I
(Merry Christmas! Here, Father, take your package) misunderstand it!
Merry Christmas, Uncle Leon! yes, here is your package too.

I misunderstand Renaissance life; I misunderstand:
The Renaissance;
Ancient China;
The Middle Atlantic States and what they are like;
The tubes of London and what they mean;
Titian, Michelangelo, Vermeer;
The origins of words;
What others are talking about;
Music from the beginnings to the present time;
Laughter; and tears, even more so;

Value (economic and esthetic);
Snow (and weather in the country);
The meaning of the symbols and myths of Christmas.
I misunderstand you,
I misunderstand the day we walked down the street together for ten
      hours—
Where were we going? I had thought we were going somewhere. I
      believe I misunderstand many of the places we passed and things
      you said . . .
I misunderstand "Sons of Burgundy,"
I misunderstand that you had nothing painted beneath your bodice,
I misunderstand "Notification of Arrival or Departure to Be Eradi-
      cated Before Affection of Deceased Tenant."
I understand that
The smoke and the clouds are both a part of the day, but

I misunderstand the words "After Departure,"
I misunderstand nothingness;
I misunderstand the attitude of people in pharmacies, on the decks of
      ships, in my bedroom, amid the pine needles, on mountains of
      cotton, everywhere—
When they say paralytic I hear parasite, and when they say coffee I
      think music . . .
What is wrong with me from head to toe
That I misinterpret everything I hear? I misunderstand:
French: often;
Italian: sometimes, almost always—for example, if someone says,
      "Fortunate ones!" I am likely to think he is referring to the
      fountain with blue and red water (I am likely to make this mis-
      take also in English).
I misunderstand Greek entirely;
I find ancient Greece very hard to understand: I probably misunder-
      stand it;

I misunderstand spoken German about 98% of the time, like the
      cathedral in the middle of a town;
I misunderstand "Beautiful Adventures"; I also think I probably
      misunderstand *La Nausée* by Jean-Paul Sartre . . .
I probably misunderstand misunderstanding itself—I misunderstand

the Via Margutta in Rome, or Via della Vite, no matter what
    street, all of them.
I misunderstand wood in the sense of its relationship to the tree; I
    misunderstand people who take one attitude or another about
    it . . .
Spring I would like to say I understand, but I most probably don't—
    autumn, winter, and summer are all in the same boat
(Ruined ancient cities by the sea).

I misunderstand *vacation* and *umbrella,*
I misunderstand *motion* and *weekly*
(Though I think I understand "Daytime Pissarros"
And the octagon—I do not understand the public garden) . . .

Oh I am sure there is a use for all of them, but what is it?
My misunderstandings confuse Rome and Ireland, and can you
Bring that beautiful sex to bear upon it?
I misunderstand what I am saying, though not to you;
I misunderstand a large boat: that is a ship.
What you are feeling for me I misunderstand totally; I think I mis-
    understand the very possibilities of feeling,
Especially here in Rome, where I somehow think I am.
I see the sky, and sails.
(I misunderstand the mustard and the bottle)
Oh that we could go sailing in that sky!

What tune came with the refreshments?
I am unable to comprehend why they were playing off key.
Is it because they wanted us to jump over the cliff
Or was one of them a bad or untrained musician
Or the whole lot of them?
At any rate
San Giovanni in Laterano
Also resisted my questioning
And turned a deaf blue dome to me
Far too successfully.

I cannot understand why you walk forwards and backwards with me.

I think it is because you want to try out your shoes for their toes.
It is Causation that is my greatest problem
And after that the really attentive study of millions of details.

I love you, but it is difficult to stop writing.
As a flea could write the Divine Comedy of a water jug. Now Irish
    mists close in upon us.
Peat sails through the air, and greenness becomes bright. Are you the
    ocean or the island? Am I on Irish soil, or are your waves cover-
    ing me?
St. Peter's bells are ringing: "Earthquake, inundation, and sleep to
    the understanding!"
(American Express! flower vendors! your beautiful straight nose! that
    delightful trattoria in Santa Maria in Trastevere!)
Let us have supper at Santa Maria in Trastevere
Where by an absolute and total misunderstanding (but not fatal) I
    once ate before I met you.
I am probably misinterpreting your answer, since I hear nothing, and
    I believe I am alone.

THE LOST FEED*

Seven actresses, impersonating hens and chickens, should, while re-
taining their human modesty and dignity, act out in as chicken-like
a way as possible the drama of the lost feed. The feed for the day
is missing. None of the hens or chickens present is responsible for
the absence of the feed, but each one suspects that some one of the
others on-stage may be the culprit. Whatever the hens and chickens
do, they should make no strictly *personal* remarks when they accuse
one another. Their accusations should be rather flat and rather gen-
eral, accusations which could be leveled at anybody about just about
anything. Chicken life is not thought to be very differentiated. After
the chickens and hens have been arguing for a long time, the feed
should be brought in and given to them.

*This and the following text are scenarios for improvisational dramas. It was the
editor's decision to anthologize them as poems. (J.H.)

THE GOLD STANDARD

A Mountain Shrine, in China. Two Monks enter, and try, without the slightest success, to explain the gold standard to each other, for four hours. There should be nothing comical whatsoever in anything they say. The drama should be allowed as a "field day" for the lighting technician, who should be allowed, and even encouraged, to make as many changes of lighting to show time of day, season, atmosphere, and mood as he deems fitting so as to make the play as beautiful and meaningful as it can possibly be. The play should end with a snowfall and with the exit of the Monks.

Jay MacPherson

MERMAID

The fish-tailed lady offering her breast
Has nothing else to give.
She'll render only brine, if pressed,
That none can drink and live.

She has a magic glass, whose spell
Makes bone look wondrous white.
By day she sings, though, travellers like to tell,
She weeps at night.

EVE IN REFLECTION

Painful and brief the act. Eve on the barren shore
Sees every cherished feature, plumed tree, bright grass,
Fresh spring, the beasts as placid as before
Beneath the inviolable glass.

There the lost girl gone under sea
Tends her undying grove, never raising her eyes
To where on the salt shell beach in revery
The mother of all living lies.

The beloved face is lost from sight,
Marred in a whelming tide of blood:
And Adam walks in the cold night
Wilderness, waste wood.

THE MARRIAGE OF EARTH AND HEAVEN

Earth draws her breath so gently, heaven bends
On her so bright a look, I could believe
That the renewal of the world was come,
The marriage of kind Earth and splendid Heaven.

'O happy pair'—the blind man lifts his harp
Down from the peg—but wait, but check the song.
The two you praise still matchless lie apart,
Thin air drawn sharp between queen Earth and Heaven.

Though I stand and stretch my hands forever
Till my hair grows down my back and my skirt to my ankles,
I shall not hear the triumphs of their trumpets
Calling the hopeful in from all the quarters
To the marriage of kind Earth and splendid Heaven.

Yet out of reason's reach a place is kept
For great occasions, with a fat four-poster bed
And a revelling-ground and a fountain showering beer
And a fiddler fiddling fine for folly's children
To riot rings around at the famous wedding
Of queen Earth and her fancy-fellow Heaven.

ORDINARY PEOPLE IN THE LAST DAYS

My mother was taken up to heaven in a pink cloud.
She was talking to a friend on the telephone
When we saw her depart through the ceiling
Still murmuring about bridge.

My father prophesied.
He looked out from behind his newspaper

And said, 'Johnny-Boy will win the Derby'.
The odds against were fifteen to one, and he won.

The unicorn yielded to my sweetheart.
She was giggling with some girls
When the unicorn walked carefully up to her
And laid his head in her lap.

The white bull ran away with my sister.
My father sent me to find her
But the oracle maundered on about a cow
And I came home disgruntled.

The dove descended on my brother.
He was working in the garden
When the air became too bright for comfort
And the glory of the bird scorched his roses.

A mouse ran away in my wainscot.
I study all day and pray all night.
My God, send me a sign of Thy coming
Or let me die.

My mother was taken up to heaven in a pink cloud,
My father prophesied,
The unicorn yielded to my sweetheart,
The white bull ran away with my sister,
The dove descended on my brother,
And a mouse ran away in my wainscot.

SIBYLLA

God Phoebus was a merry lad,
Courted my mother's daughter:
Said I, 'To swim I'll be quite glad,
But keep me from the water.'

He swore he'd break my looking-glass
And dock my maiden tresses;
He told me tales of many a pass,
All of them successes.

There's other ways to catch a god
Who's feeling gay and girly
Than tickling with a fishing-rod
Among the short and curly.

I took his gift and thwarted him,
I listened to his vows, and
Though looks are gone and eyes grow dim,
I'll live to be a thousand.

I'm mercifully rid of youth,
No callers plague me ever:
I'm virtuous, I tell the truth—
And you can see I'm clever!

O FENIX CULPA

The wicked Phoenix in her baleful fires
Here on this ground suspires.
What God has put asunder here combines
And viprish intertwines.
Duplicity of head and heart
Has taught her lust that art.
Not strength and sweetness in one frame,
Dying and rising still the same:
Her charnel and her marriage-bed,
The womb that her own being bred
—Strains to rise and cannot fly,
Looks to death and may not die,
Writhes on griefs beyond recall
And shall, till doomfire burn all.

THE PLOWMAN IN DARKNESS

You ask for the Plowman:
He's as much
In the dark as you are,
Moves by touch,
Stubbing his toes
From age to age
Is working up a
Snorting rage,
Swears he'll beat his plowshare
Into a sword
Come the great and harrowing
Day of the Lord.

THE GARDEN OF THE SEXES

I have a garden closed away
And shadowed from the light of day
Where Love hangs bound on every tree
And I alone go free.

His sighs, that turn the weathers round,
His tears, that water all the ground,
His blood, that reddens in the vine,
These all are mine.

At night the golden apple-tree
Is my fixed station, whence I see
Terrible, sublime and free,
My loves go wheeling over me.

THE UNICORN-TREE

Bound and weeping, but with smiles
To keep herself from scorn,
The lady of the tree beguiles
The wrathful unicorn.

What anger in the springing wood
Or coil along the bough
Flushes the milky skin with blood?
Too late to question now.

The hunters with their kill are gone.
The darkening tree again
Arches its wicked length upon
The virgin in her chain.

THE BOATMAN

You might suppose it easy
For a maker not too lazy
To convert the gentle reader to an Ark:
But it takes a willing pupil
To admit both gnat and camel
—Quite an eyeful, all the crew that must embark.

After me when comes the deluge
And you're looking round for refuge
From God's anger pouring down in gush and spout,
Then you take the tender creature
—You remember, that's the reader—
And you pull him through his navel inside out.

That's to get his beasts outside him,
For they've got to come aboard him,

As the best directions have it, two by two.
When you've taken all their tickets
And you've marched them through his sockets,
Let the tempest bust Creation: heed not you.

For you're riding high and mighty
In a gale that's pushing ninety
With a solid bottom under you—that's his.
Fellow flesh affords a rampart,
And you've got along for comfort
All the world there ever shall be, was, and is.

THE BEAUTY OF JOB'S DAUGHTERS

The old, the mad, the blind have fairest daughters.
Take Job: the beasts the accuser sends at evening
Shoulder his house and shake it; he's not there,
Attained in age to inwardness of daughters,
In all the land no women found so fair.

Angels and sons of God are nearest neighbours,
And even the accuser may repair
To walk with Job in pleasures of his daughters:
Wide shining rooms more warmly lit at evening,
Gardens beyond whose secrets scent the air.

Not wiles of men nor envy of the neighbours,
Riches of earth, nor what heaven holds more rare,
Can take from Job the beauty of his daughters,
The gardens in the rock, music at evening,
And cup so full that all who come must share.

Perhaps we passed them? it was late, or evening,
And surely those were desert stumps, not daughters,
In fact we doubt that they were ever there.
The old, the mad, the blind have fairest daughters.
In all the land no women found so fair.

James Merrill

MIRROR

I grow old under an intensity
Of questioning looks. *Nonsense,*
I try to say, *I cannot teach you children
How to live.—If not you, who will?*
Cries one of them aloud, grasping my gilded
Frame till the world sways. *If not you, who will?*
Between their visits the table, its arrangement
Of Bible, fern and Paisley, all past change,
Does very nicely. If ever I feel curious
As to what others endure,
Across the parlor *you* provide examples,
Wide open, sunny, of everything I am
Not. You embrace a whole world without once caring
To set it in order. That takes thought. Out there
Something is being picked. The red-and-white bandannas
Go to my heart. A fine young man
Rides by on horseback. Now the door shuts. Hester
Confides in me her first unhappiness.
This much, you see, would never have been fitted
Together, but for me. Why then is it
They more and more neglect me? Late one sleepless
Midsummer night I strained to keep
Five tapers from your breathing. *No,* the widowed
Cousin said, *Let them go out.* I did.
The room brimmed with gray sound, all the instreaming
Muslin of your dream . . .
Years later now, two of the grown grandchildren
Sit with novels face-down on the sill,
Content to muse upon your tall transparence,
Your clouds, brown fields, persimmon far
And cypress near. One speaks. *How superficial*

186

Appearances are! Since then, as if a fish
Had broken the perfect silver of my reflectiveness,
I have lapses. I suspect
Looks from behind, where nothing is, cool gazes
Through the blind flaws of my mind. As days,
As decades lengthen, this vision
Spreads and blackens. I do not know whose it is,
But I think it watches for my last silver
To blister, flake, float leaf by life, each milling-
Downward dumb conceit, to a standstill
From which not even you strike any brilliant
Chord in me, and to a faceless will,
Echo of mine, I am amenable.

THE BROKEN HOME

Crossing the street,
I saw the parents and the child
At their window, gleaming like fruit
With evening's mild gold leaf.

In a room on the floor below,
Sunless, cooler—a brimming
Saucer of wax, marbly and dim—
I have lit what's left of my life.

I have thrown out yesterday's milk
And opened a book of maxims.
The flame quickens. The word stirs.

Tell me, tongue of fire,
That you and I are as real
At least as the people upstairs.

My father, who had flown in World War I,
Might have continued to invest his life

In cloud banks well above Wall Street and wife.
But the race was run below, and the point was to win.

Too late now, I make out in his blue gaze
(Through the smoked glass of being thirty-six)
The soul eclipsed by twin black pupils, sex
And business; time was money in those days.

Each thirteenth year he married. When he died
There were already several chilled wives
In sable orbit—rings, cars, permanent waves.
We'd felt him warming up for a green bride.

He could afford it. He was "in his prime"
At three score ten. But money was not time.

When my parents were younger this was a popular act:
A veiled woman would leap from an electric, wine-dark car
To the steps of no matter what—the Senate or the
          Ritz Bar—
And bodily, at newsreel speed, attack

No matter whom—Al Smith or José Maria Sert
Or Clemenceau—veins standing out on her throat
As she yelled *War mongerer! Pig! Give us the vote!*,
And would have to be hauled away in her hobble skirt.

What had the man done? Oh, made history.
Her business (he had implied) was giving birth,
Tending the house, mending the socks.

Always that same old story—
Father Time and Mother Earth,
A marriage on the rocks.

One afternoon, red, satyr-thighed
Michael, the Irish setter, head

Passionately lowered, led
The child I was to a shut door. Inside,

Blinds beat sun from the bed.
The green-gold room throbbed like a bruise.
Under a sheet, clad in taboos
Lay whom we sought, her hair undone, outspread,

And of a blackness found, if ever now, in old
Engravings where the acid bit.
I must have needed to touch it
Or the whiteness—was she dead?
Her eyes flew open, startled strange and cold.
The dog slumped to the floor. She reached for me. I fled.

Tonight they have stepped out onto the gravel.
The party is over. It's the fall
Of 1931. They love each other still.

She: Charlie, I can't stand the pace.
He: Come on, honey—why, you'll bury us all!

A lead soldier guards my windowsill:
Khaki rifle, uniform, and face.
Something in me grows heavy, silvery, pliable.

How intensely people used to feel!
Like metal poured at the close of a proletarian novel,
Refined and glowing from the crucible,
I see those two hearts, I'm afraid,
Still. Cool here in the graveyard of good and evil,
They are even so to be honored and obeyed.

. . . Obeyed, at least, inversely. Thus
I rarely buy a newspaper, or vote.
To do so, I have learned, is to invite
The tread of a stone guest within my house.

Shooting this rusted bolt, though, against him,
I trust I am no less time's child than some
Who on the heath impersonate Poor Tom
Or on the barricades risk life and limb.

Nor do I try to keep a garden, only
An avocado in a glass of water—
Roots pallid, gemmed with air. And later,

When the small gilt leaves have grown
Fleshy and green, I let them die, yes, yes,
And start another. I am earth's no less.

A child, a red dog roam the corridors,
Still, of the broken home. No sound. The brilliant
Rag runners halt before wide-open doors.
My old room! Its wallpaper—cream, medallioned
With pink and brown—brings back the first nightmares,
Long summer colds, and Emma, sepia-faced,
Perspiring over broth carried upstairs
Aswim with golden fats I could not taste.

The real house became a boarding-school.
Under the ballroom ceiling's allegory
Someone at last may actually be allowed
To learn something; or, from my window, cool
With the unstiflement of the entire story,
Watch a red setter stretch and sink in cloud.

FROM THE CUPOLA

for H.M.

The sister who told fortunes prophesied
A love-letter. In the next mail it came.
You didn't recognize the writer's name
And wondered he knew yours. Ah well. That seed

Has since become a world of blossom and bark.
The letters fill a drawer, the gifts a room.
No hollow of your day is hidden from
His warm concern. Still you are in the dark.

Too much understanding petrifies.
The early letters struck you as blackmail.
You have them now by heart, a rosy veil
Colors the phrase repaired to with shut eyes.

Was the time always wrong for you to meet?—
Not that he ever once proposed as much.
Your sisters joke about it. "It's too rich!
Somebody Up There loves you, Psyche sweet."

Tell me about him, then. Not a believer,
I'll hold my tongue while you, my dear, dictate.
Him I have known too little (or, of late,
Too well) to trust my own view of your lover.

Oh but one has many, many tongues!
And you will need a certain smouldering five
Deep in the ash of something I survive,
Poke and rummage with as reluctant tongs

As possible. The point won't be to stage
One of our torchlit hunts for truth. Truth asks
Just this once to sleep with fiction, masks
Of tears and laughter on the moonstruck page;

To cauterize what babbles to be healed—
Just this once not by candor. Here and now,
Psyche, I quench that iron lest it outglow
A hovering radiance your fingers shield.

Renaissance features grafted onto Greek
Revival, glassed, hexagonal lookouts crown
Some of the finest houses in this town.
By day or night, cloud, sunbeam, lunatic streak,

They alternately ravish and disown
Earth, sky, and water— Are you with me? Speak.

SUNLIGHT   Crossfire
of rays and shadows each
glancing off a windowpane a stone
You alone my correspondent

have remained sheer
projection   Hurt   Not gravely   Not at all
Your bloodlessness a glaze
of thin thin varnish where I kneel

Were the warm drop
upon your letter oil and were that page
your sleeping person then
all would indeed be lost

Our town is small
its houses built like temples
The rare stranger I let pass with lowered
eyes   He also could be you

Nights the last red
wiped from my lips the harbor
blinking out gem by gem how utterly
we've been undressed

You will not come
to the porch at noon will you rustling your wings
or masked as crone or youth
The mouths behind our faces kiss

Kindlings of truth
Risen from the dawn mist
some wriggling silver in a tern's beak scrawls
joyous memoranda onto things

TODAY I have your letter from the South
where as a child I   but of course you know
Three times I've read it at my attic window
A city named for palms half mummy and half myth
pools flashing talking birds the world of my
first vision of you Psyche   Though it's May

that could be frost upon the apple trees
silvery plump as sponges above the pale
arm of the Sound and the pane is chill to feel
I live now by the seasons burn and freeze
far from that world where nothing changed or died
unless to be reborn on the next tide

You daylong in the saddles of foaming opal
ride   I am glad   Come dusk lime juice and gin
deepen the sunset under your salt skin
I've tasted that side of the apple
A city named for palms half desert and half dream
its dry gold settles on my mouth   I bloom

Where nothing died   Breaking on us like waves
the bougainvillea bloomed fell bloomed again
The new sea wall rose from the hurricane
and no less staunchly from the old freed slave's
ashes each night her grandchild climbed the stairs
to twitch white gauze across the stinging stars

City half dream half desert where at dawn
the sprinkler dervish whirled and all was crystalline
within each house half brothel and half shrine
up from the mirror tabletop had flown
by noon the shadow of each plate each spoon to float
in light that warbled on the ceiling   Wait

ALICE has entered talking

Any mirage if seen from a remote stand
point is refreshing   Yes but dust and heat

lie at its heart   Poor Psyche you forget
That was a cruel impossible wonderland

The very sidewalks suffered   Ours that used
to lead can you remember to the beach
I felt it knew and waited for us each
morning to trot its length in teardrop punctured shoes

when in fact the poor dumb thing lay I now know
under a dark spell cast from quite another
quarter the shadow of a towering mother
smooth as stone and thousandbreasted though

her milk was watery scant so much for love
false like everything in that whole world
However   This shadow that a royal palm hurled
onto the sidewalk from ten yards above

day night rustling and wrestling never shattered
except to mend back forth or lost its grip
the batwing offspring of her ladyship
Our orchid stucco house looked on greenshuttered

stoic   But the sidewalk suffered most
Like somebody I shall not name it lacked
perspective   It failed absolutely to detect
the root of all that evil   The clues it missed

Nights after a windstorm great yellow paper
dry branches lying on the curb in heaps
like fancy dress don't ask me whose someone who steps
forth and is changed by the harsh moonlight to vapor

the sidewalk could only grit itself and shift
Some mornings respite   A grisaille opaque
as poured concrete   And yet by ten o'clock
the phantom struck again in a first sunshaft

Off to the beach   Us nurse in single file

Those days we'd meet our neighbor veiled and hatted
tanagra leading home out of the sun she hated
a little boy with water wings   We'd smile

then hold our breaths to pass a barricade
of black smells rippling up from the soft hot
brink of the mirage past which sidewalks could not
follow   Ours stood there crumbling then obeyed

a whisper back of it and turned   The sea the loose
unshadowed sand too free white heterodox
ever to be congealed into sidewalks
ours never saw GIVE ME THE SNAPPED SHOELACE

LIZARDS ANTS SCRAPS OF SILVER FOIL
hoarse green tongues begged from each new crack   No use
The shadow trod it as our nightmares us
Then we moved here where gray skies are the rule

What   Why not simply have cut down the tree
Psyche I can't believe my   Hush   You child
Cut down the   I've got gooseflesh   Feel   I'm chilled
My sister's hyperthyroid eyes fix me

The whites lackluster shot with miniature
red brambles abruptly glitter overspill
down powdered cheeks   Alice can weep at will
How to convey the things I feel for her

She is more strange than Iceland bathed all night
an invalid in sunshine   Lava cliffs
The geyser that erupts the loon that laughs
I move to kiss her but she hums a note

and licks her lips   *Well darling I must fly*
before you read what it does not intend
about yourself and your mysterious friend
say or some weird rivalry that I

may once have harbored though I harbor none
now nor does Gertrude not the tiniest pang
into this long but kindly meant harangue
She nods and leaves the room   And I am here alone

I place the ladder hoist from rung to rung
my pail and cloths into a cupola glassed
entirely with panes some tinted amethyst
it is my task to clean   Up here among

spatterings and reflections wipe as I will
these six horizons still the rain's dry ghost
and my own features haunt the roofs the coast
How does one get to know a landscape well

When did we leave the South   Why do we live indoors
I wonder sweating to the cadence   Even
on sunless days the cupola is an oven
Views blur   This thing we see them through endures

MIDNIGHT   I dream I dream   The slow moon eludes
one stilled cloud   Din of shimmerings   From across the Sound
what may have begun as no more
than a willow's sleepwalking outline quickens detaches
comes to itself in the cupola
panics from pane to pane and then impulsively
surrendering fluttering by now the sixteenfold
wings of the cherubim unclipped by faith or reason
stands there my dream made whole
over whose walls again
a red vine black in moonlight crawls
made habitable   Each cell of the concrete
fills with sweet light   The wave breaks
into tears   Come if its you   Step down
to where I   Stop   For at your touch the dream

cracks the angel tenses flees

NOON finds me faced by a small troop of furies
They are my senses shrill and ominous
We who were trained they cry *to do your pleasure
are kept like children   Is this fair to us*

Dear ones I say bending to kiss their faces
*trust me   One day you'll understand   Meanwhile
suppose we think of things to raise our spirits*
and leading the two easiest to beguile

into the kitchen feed them shots of Bourbon
Their brother who loves Brahms conceives a wish
for gems from L'Africana played at volumes
that make the dwarf palm shudder in its dish

The pale one with your eyes restively flashing
takes in the dock the ashen Sound the sky
The fingers of the eldest brush my features
But you are smiling she says coldly   *Why*

STAR or candle being lit
    but to shed itself
into blackness partly night's
sure that no less golden warm than it
        is our love
will have missed the truth by half
We see according to our lights

Eros   husband   names distort
    you who have no name
Peace upon your neophytes
Help me when the christenings shall start
        o my love
to defend your sleep from them
and see according to our lights

Ah and should discernment's twin
    tyrants adamant
for their meal of pinks and whites
be who call those various torches in
        help me love
This is nothing I shall want
We see according to our lights

When as written you have lapsed
    back into the god
darts and wings and appetites
what of him the lover all eclipsed
        by sheer love
Shut my eyes it does no good
Who will ever put to rights

Psyche, hush. This is me, James.
    Writing lest he think
Of the reasons why he writes—
Boredom, fear, mixed vanities and shames;
        Also love.
From my phosphorescent ink
Trickle faint unworldly lights

Down your face. Come, we'll both rest.
    Weeping? You must not.
All our pyrotechnic flights
Miss the sleeper in the pitch-dark breast.
        He is love:
He is everyone's blind spot.
We see according to our lights.

"What's that sound? Is it you, dear?"
"Yes. I was just eating something."
"What?"
"I don't know—I mean, an apricot . . ."
"Hadn't you best switch on the light and make sure?"
"No, thank you, Gertrude."
A hurt silence ensued.

"Oh, Psyche!" her sister burst out at length. "Here you are, surrounded by loving kin, in a house crammed with lovely old things, and what do you crave but the unfamiliar, the 'transcendental'? I declare, you're turning into the classic New England old maid!"

. . . .

Psyche's hands dropped from her wet, white face. The time had come—except that Time, like Love, wears a mask in this story, whose action requires perhaps thirty-six hours of Spring, perhaps thirty-six Springs of a life—a moment nevertheless had come to take the electric torch and leave her sisters without a word. Later she was to recall a tear-streaked muzzle, the marvelous lashed golds of an iris reflecting her own person backed by ever tinier worlds of moonlight and tossing palms, then, at the center, blackness, a fixed point, a spindle on which everything had begun to turn. Piercing her to the brain.

Spelt out in brutal prose, all had been plain.

RAIN Evening The drive in My sisters' gold sedan's
  eyes have gone dim and dark windows are sealed
    For vision's sake two wipers wield
  the automatic coquetry of fans

In the next car young Eros and his sweetheart sit
  fire and saltwater still from their embrace
    Grief plays upon his sated face
  Her mask of tears does not exactly fit

The love goddess his mother overflows a screen
  sixty feet wide or seems to Who can plumb
    those motes of rose and platinum
  At once they melt back into the machine

throbbing dry and dispassionate beyond our ken
  to spool her home whose beauty flabbergasts
    The nervous systems of her guests
  drink and drink the sparkling staleness in

Now in her element steam she looms up from a bath
   The hero's breastplate mirrors her red lips
      It burns and clouds   As waterdrops
  course down the monumental cheeks of both

they kiss   My sisters turn on me from either side
   shrieking with glee under the rainlight mask
      fondle and pinch in mean burlesque
  of things my angel you and I once tried

In no time he alone is left of a proud corps
   That dustcloud hides triumphant fleeing Huns
      Lips parched by a montage of suns
  he cannot taste our latter night's downpour

while she by now my sisters fatten upon fact
   is on location in Djakarta where
      tomorrow's sun illumines her
  emoting in strange arms   It's all an act

Eros are you like her so false a naked glance
   turns you into that slackjawed fleshproud youth
      driving away   Was he your truth
  Is it too late to study ignorance

These fictive lives these loves of the comedian
   so like so unlike ours which hurt and heal
      are what the gods know   You can feel
  lust and fulfillment Eros no more than

ocean its salt depths or uranium its hot
   disintegrative force or I our fable
      My interest like the rain grown feeble
  a film of sorrow on my eyes they shut

I may already be part god   Asleep awake
   some afterglow as of a buried heaven
      keeps flickering through me   I may even
  learn to love it Eros for your sake

MORNING   The task is done   When my sisters wake
they will look once more upon pale water and clear sky
a fair far brow of land
with its fillet of Greek trees oak apple willow
and here below in the foreground
across a street finished down to the last detail
a red clapboard temple   The neat outlines
it's a warehouse really have been filled with colors
dull red flaking walls   white trim
and pediment   tar roof patched black on black
Greek colors   An effect I hope
not too much spoiled by a big yellow legend
BOAT WORKS on the roof which seagulls helicopters
the highup living and the happy dead
are in a position to read
Outside indeed a boat lies covered with tarpaulin
Old headlines mend a missing pane   The warehouse
seems but in the time it takes to say *abandoned*
a face male old molepale in sun
though blinded by the mullion's shadow
has floated to an eerie scale the rising
wind flutes out of the oaken depths
I look away   When I look back
the panic's over   It is afternoon
Now the window reflects my sisters' white
mock Ionic portico and me emerging
blinking   Too bright to bear or turn from
spring's first real sun burns on the numb blue Sound
Beyond the warehouse past the round GULF sign
whose warning it ignores a baby dock has waded
The small waves stretch their necks gulls veer and scold
I walk the length of our Greek Revival village
from library to old blind lighthouse
Like one entranced who talks as awake she cannot
a potpourri of dead chalkpetal dialects
dead anyhow all winter
lips caulked with faded pollen and dust of cloves
I find that I can break the cipher
come to light along certain humming branches

make out not only *apple blossom* and *sun*
but perfectly the dance of darker undertones
on pavement or white wall   It is this dance I know
that cracks the pavement   I do know
Finally I reach a garden where I am to uproot
the last parsnips for my sisters' dinner
Not parsnips mastodons   But this year's greens
already frill them and they pull easily
from the soft ground   Two of the finest
are tightly interlocked have grown that way   They lie
united in the grave of sunny air
as in their breathing living dark
I look at them a long while
mealy and soiled in one another's arms
and blind full to the ivory marrow
with tender blindness   Then I bury them
once more in memory of us
Back home   Gold skies   My basket full
Lifting it indoor I turn   The little dock
It is out there still on stilts in freezing water
It must know by now
that no one is coming after it that it must wait
for morning for next week for summer
by which time it will have silvered and splintered
and the whitewinged boats and the bridegroom's burning sandals
will come too late   It's dark   It's dinner time
Light the lamp my sisters call from where they eat
There follows a hushed preening and straining
wallpaper horsehair glass wood pewter glue
Now is their moment when all else goes black
and what is there but substance to turn to
Sister the lamp   The round
moon mallet has risen and struck   Of the warehouse pulverized
one faintest blueprint glimmers by which to build it
on the same spot tomorrow somehow right
Light your lamp Psyche dear
My hand is on the switch   I have done this
faithfully each night since the first
Tonight I think will not be different

Then soft light lights the room the furniture
a blush invades even the dropped lid
yes and I am here alone
I and my flesh and blood

Thank you, Psyche. I should think those panes
Were just about as clear as they can be.
It's time I turned my light on. Child, leave me.
Here on the earth we loved alone remains

One shrunken amphitheatre, look, to moon
Hugely above. Ranked glintings from within
Hint that a small articulate crowd has been
Gathered for days now, waiting. None too soon,

Whether in lower or in upper case,
Will come the Moment for the metal of each
To sally forth—once more into the breach!
Beyond it, glory lies, a virgin space

Acrackle in white hunger for the word.
We've seen what comes next. There is no pure deed.
A black-and-red enchanter, a deep-dyed
Coil of—No matter. One falls back, soiled, blurred.

And on the page, of course, black only. Damned
If I don't tire of the dark view of things.
I think of your 'Greek colors' and it rings
A sweet bell. Time to live! Haven't I dimmed

That portion of the ribbon—whose red glows
Bright with disuse—sufficiently for a bit?
Tomorrow mayn't I start to pay my debt,
In wine, in heart's blood, to la vie en rose?

This evening it will do to be alone,
Here, with your girlish figures: parsnip, Eros,

Shadow, blossom, windowpane. The warehouse.
The lamp I smell in every other line.

Do you smell mine? From its rubbed brass a moth
Hurtles in motes and tatters of itself
—Be careful, tiny sister, drabbest sylph!—
Against the hot glare, the consuming myth,

Drops, and is still. My hands move. An intense,
Slow-paced, erratic dance goes on below.
I have received from whom I do not know
These letters. Show me, light, if they make sense.

AN URBAN CONVALESCENCE

Out for a walk, after a week in bed,
I find them tearing up part of my block
And, chilled through, dazed and lonely, join the dozen
In meek attitudes, watching a huge crane
Fumble luxuriously in the filth of years.
Her jaws dribble rubble. An old man
Laughs and curses in her brain,
Bringing to mind the close of *The White Goddess*.

As usual in New York, everything is torn down
Before you have had time to care for it.
Head bowed, at the shrine of noise, let me try to recall
What building stood here. Was there a building at all?
I have lived on this same street for a decade.

Wait. Yes. Vaguely a presence rises
Some five floors high, of shabby stone
—Or am I confusing it with another one
In another part of town, or of the world?—
And over its lintel into focus vaguely
Misted with blood (my eyes are shut)
A single garland sways, stone fruit, stone leaves,

Which years of grit had etched until it thrust
Roots down, even into the poor soil of my seeing.
When did the garland become part of me?
I ask myself, amused almost,
Then shiver once from head to toe,

Transfixed by a particular cheap engraving of garlands
Bought for a few francs long ago,
All calligraphic tendril and cross-hatched rondure,
Ten years ago, and crumpled up to stanch
Boughs dripping, whose white gestures filled a cab,
And thought of neither then nor since.
Also, to clasp them, the small, red-nailed hand
Of no one I can place. Wait. No. Her name, her features
Lie toppled underneath that year's fashions.
The words she must have spoken, setting her face
To fluttering like a veil, I cannot hear now,
Let alone understand.

So that I am already on the stair,
As it were, of where I lived,
When the whole structure shudders at my tread
And soundlessly collapses, filling
The air with motes of stone.
Onto the still erect building next door
Are pressed levels and hues—
Pocked rose, streaked greens, brown whites.
Who drained the pousse-café?
Wires and pipes, snapped off at the roots, quiver.

Well, that is what life does. I stare
A moment longer, so. And presently
The massive volume of the world
Closes again.

Upon that book I swear
To abide by what it teaches:
Gospels of ugliness and waste,
Of towering voids, of soiled gusts,

Of a shrieking to be faced
Full into, eyes astream with cold—

With cold?
All right then. With self-knowledge.

Indoors at last, the pages of *Time* are apt
To open, and the illustrated mayor of New York,
Given a glimpse of how and where I work,
To note yet one more house that can be scrapped.

Unwillingly I picture
My walls weathering in the general view.
It is not even as though the new
Buildings did very much for architecture.

Suppose they did. The sickness of our time requires
That these as well be blasted in their prime.
You would think the simple fact of having lasted
Threatened our cities like mysterious fires.

There are certain phrases which to use in a poem
Is like rubbing silver with quicksilver. Bright
But facile, the glamour deadens overnight.
For instance, how 'the sickness of our time'

Enhances, then debases, what I feel.
At my desk I swallow in a glass of water
No longer cordial, scarcely wet, a pill
They had told me not to take until much later.

With the result that back into my imagination
The city glides, like cities seen from the air,
Mere smoke and sparkle to the passenger
Having in mind another destination

Which now is not that honey-slow descent
Of the Champs-Elysées, her hand in his,
But the dull need to make some kind of house
Out of the life lived, out of the love spent.

W. S. Merwin

WHITE GOAT, WHITE RAM

The gaiety of three winds is a game of green
Shining, of grey-and-gold play in the holly-bush
Among the rocks on the hill-side, and if ever
The earth was shaken, say a moment ago
Or whenever it came to be, only the leaves and the spread
Sea still betray it, trembling; and their tale betides
The faintest of small voices, almost still.
A road winds among the grey rocks, over the hill,
Arrives from out of sight, from nowhere we know,
Of an uncertain colour; and she stands at the side
Nearer the sea, not far from the brink, legs straddled wide
Over the swinging udder, her back and belly
Slung like a camp of hammocks, her head raised,
The narrow jaw grinding sideways, ears flapping sideways,
Eyes wide apart like the two moons of Mars
At their opposing. So broadly is she blind
Who has no names to see with: over her shoulder
She sees not summer, not the idea of summer,
But green meanings, shadows, the gold light of now, familiar,
The sense of long day-warmth, of sparse grass in the open
Game of the winds; an air that is plenitude,
Describing itself in no name; all known before,
Perceived many times before, yet not
Remembered, or at most felt as usual. Even the kids,
Grown now and gone, are forgotten,
As though by habit. And he on the other side
Of the road, hooves braced among spurge and asphodel,
Tears the grey grass at its roots, his massive horns
Tossing delicately, as by long habit, as by
Habit learned, or without other knowledge

And without question inherited, or found
As first he found the air, the first daylight, first milk at the tetter,
The paths, the pen, the seasons. They are white, these two,
As we should say those are white who remember nothing,
And we for our uses call that innocence,
So that our gracelessness may have the back of a goat
To ride away upon; so that when our supreme gesture
Of propitiation has obediently been raised
It may be the thicket-snared ram that dies instead of the son;
So even that we may frame the sense that is now
Into a starred figure of last things, of our own
End, and there by these beasts know ourselves
One from another: some to stay in the safety
Of the rock, but many on the other hand
To be dashed over the perilous brink. There is no need
Even that they should be gentle, for us to use them
To signify gentleness, for us to lift them as a sign
Invoking gentleness, conjuring by their shapes
The shape of our desire, which without them would remain
Without a form and nameless. For our uses
Also are a dumbness, a mystery,
Which like a habit stretches ahead of us
And was here before us; so, again, we use these
To designate what was before us, since we cannot
See it in itself, for who can recognize
And call by true names, familiarly, the place
Where before this he was, though for nine months
Or the world's full age he housed there? Yet it seems
That by such a road, arriving from out of sight,
From nowhere we know, we may have come, and these
Figure as shapes we may have been. Only, to them
The road is less than a road, though it divides them,
A bit of flat space merely, perhaps not even
A thing that leads elsewhere, except when they
Are driven along it, for direction is to them
The paths their own preference and kinds have made
And follow: routes through no convenience
And world of ours, but through their own sense
And mystery. Mark this; for though they assume

Now the awkward postures of illustrations
For all our parables, yet the mystery they stand in
Is still as far from what they signify
As from the mystery we stand in. It is the sign
We make of them, not they, that speaks from their dumbness
That our dumbness may speak. There in the thin grass
A few feet away they browse beyond words; for a mystery
Is that for which we have not yet received
Or made the name, the terms, that may enclose
And call it. And by virtue of such we stand beyond
Earthquake and wind and burning, and all the uncovenanted
Terror of becoming, and beyond the small voice; and on
Another hand, as it were a little above us
There are the angels. We are dumb before them, and move
In a different mystery; but may there be
Another road we do not see as a road: straight, narrow,
Or broad or the sector of a circle, or perhaps
All these, where without knowing it we stand
On one side or another? I have known such a way
But at moments only, and when it seemed I was driven
Along it, and along no other that my preference
Or kind had made. And of these others above us
We know only the whisper of an elusive sense,
Infrequent meanings and shadows, analogies
With light and the beating of wings. Yet now, perhaps only
A few feet away in the shaking leaves they wait
Beyond our words, beyond earthquake, whirlwind, fire,
And all the uncovenanted terror of becoming,
And beyond the small voice. Oh we cannot know and we are not
What we signify, but in what sign
May we be innocent, for out of our dumbness
We would speak for them, give speech to the mute tongues
Of angels. Listen: more than the sea's thunder
Foregathers in the grey cliffs; the roots of our hair
Stir like the leaves of the holly bush where now
Not games the wind ponders, but impatient
Glories, fire: and we go stricken suddenly
Humble, and the covering of our feet
Offends, for the ground where we find we stand is holy.

ONE-EYE

('In the country of the blind the one-eyed man is king.')

On that vacant day
After kicking and moseying here and there
For some time, he lifted that carpet-corner
 His one eye-lid, and the dyed light
Leapt at him from all sides like dogs. Also hues
That he had never heard of, in that place
 Were bleeding and playing.

Even so, it was
Only at the grazing of light fingers
Over his face, unannounced, and then his
 Sight of many mat eyes, paired white
Irises like dried peas looking, that it dawned
On him: his sidelong idling had found
 The country of the blind.

Whose swarming digits
Knew him at once: their king, come to them
Out of a saying. And chanting an anthem
 Unto his one eye, to the dry
Accompaniment that their leaping fingers made
Flicking round him like locusts in a cloud,
 They took him home with them.

Their shapely city
Shines like a suit. On a plain chair he was set
In a cloak of hands, and crowned, to intricate
 Music. They sent him their softest
Daughters, clad only in scent and their own
Vast ears, meantime making different noises
 In each ante-chamber.

They can be wakened
Sometimes by a feather falling on the next
Floor, and they keep time by the water-clocks'
        Dropping even when they sleep. Once
He would expound to them all, from his only
Light, day breaking, the sky spiked and the
        Earth amuck with color.

        And they would listen,
Amazed at his royalty, gaping like
Sockets, and would agree, agree, blank
        As pearls. At the beginning.
Alone in brightness, soon he spoke of it
In sleep only; 'Look, look', he would call out
        In the dark only.

        Now in summer gaudy
With birds he says nothing; of their thefts, often
Beheld, and their beauties, now for a long time
        Nothing. Nothing, day after day,
To see the black thumb as big as a valley
Over their heads descending silently
        Out of a quiet sky.

THE DRUNK IN THE FURNACE

        For a good decade
The furnace stood in the naked gulley, fireless
And vacant as any hat. Then when it was
No more to them than a hulking black fossil
To erode unnoticed with the rest of the junk-hill
By the poisonous creek, and rapidly to be added
        To their ignorance,

        They were afterwards astonished
To confirm, one morning, a twist of smoke like a pale

Resurrection, staggering out of its chewed hole,
And to remark then other tokens that someone,
Cosily bolted behind the eye-holed iron
Door of the drafty burner, had there established
        His bad castle.

    Where he gets his spirits
It's a mystery. But the stuff keeps him musical:
Hammer-and-anvilling with poker and bottle
To his jugged bellowings, till the last groaning clang
As he collapses onto the rioting
Springs of a litter of car-seats ranged on the grates,
        To sleep like an iron pig.

    In their tar-paper church
On a text about stoke-holes that are sated never
Their Reverend lingers. They nod and hate trespassers.
When the furnace wakes, though, all afternoon
Their witless offspring flock like piped rats to its siren
Crescendo, and agape on the crumbling ridge
        Stand in a row and learn.

THE WAY TO THE RIVER

for Dido

The way to the river leads past the names of
Ash the sleeves the wreaths of hinges
Through the song of the bandage vendor

I lay your name by my voice
As I go

The way to the river leads past the late
Doors and the games of the children born looking backwards
They play that they are broken glass
The numbers wait in the halls and the clouds
Call

From windows
They play that they are old they are putting the horizon
Into baskets they are escaping they are
Hiding

I step over the sleepers the fires the calendars
My voice turns to you

I go past the juggler's condemned building the hollow
Windows gallery
Of invisible presidents the same motion in them all
In a parked cab by the sealed wall the hats are playing
Sort of poker with somebody's
Old snapshots game I don't understand they lose
The rivers one
After the other I begin to know where I am

I am home

Be here the flies from the house of the mapmaker
Walk on our letters I can tell
And the days hang medals between us
I have lit our room with a glove of yours be
Here I turn
To your name and the hour remembers
Its one word
Now

Be here what can we
Do for the dead the footsteps full of money
I offer you what I have my
Poverty

To the city of wires I have brought home a handful
Of water I walk slowly
In front of me they are building the empty
Ages I see them reflected not for long
Be here I am no longer ashamed of time it is too brief its hands
Have no names

I have passed it I know

    Oh Necessity you with the face you with
    All the faces

This is written on the back of everything

But we
Will read it together

IN THE NIGHT FIELDS

I heard the sparrows shouting "Eat, eat,"
And then the day dragged its carcass in back of the hill.
Slowly the tracks darkened.

The smoke rose steadily from no fires.
The old hunger, left in the old darkness,
Turned like a hanged knife.
I would have preferred a quiet life.
The bugs of regret began their services
Using my spine as a rosary. I left the maps
For the spiders.
Let's go, I said.

           Light of the heart,
The wheat had started lighting its lanterns,
And in every house in heaven there were lights waving
Hello good-bye. But that's
Another life.
Snug on the crumbling earth
The old bottles lay dreaming of new wine.
I picked up my breast, which had gone out.
By other lights I go looking for yours

Through the standing harvest of my lost arrows.

Under the moon the shadow
Practices mowing. Not for me, I say,
Please not for my
Benefit. A man cannot live by bread
Alone.

THE LAST ONE

Well they'd made up their minds to be everywhere because why not.
Everywhere was theirs because they thought so.
They with two leaves they whom the birds despise.
In the middle of stones they made up their minds.
They started to cut.

Well they cut everything because why not.
Everything was theirs because they thought so.
It fell into its shadows and they took both away.
Some to have some for burning.

Well cutting everything they came to the water.
They came to the end of the day there was one left standing.
They would cut it tomorrow they went away.
The night gathered in the last branches.
The shadow of the night gathered in the shadow on the water.
The night and the shadow put on the same head.
And it said Now.

Well in the morning they cut the last one.
Like the others the last one fell into its shadow.
It fell into its shadow on the water.
They took it away its shadow stayed on the water.

Well they shrugged they started trying to get the shadow away.
They cut right to the ground the shadow stayed whole.
They laid boards on it the shadow came out on top.
They shone lights on it the shadow got blacker and clearer.

They exploded the water the shadow rocked.
They built a huge fire on the roots.
They sent up black smoke between the shadow and the sun.
The new shadow flowed without changing the old one.

They shrugged they went away to get stones.

They came back the shadow was growing.
They started setting up stones it was growing.
They looked the other way it went on growing.
They decided they would make a stone out of it.
They took stones to the water they poured them into the shadow.
They poured them in they poured them in the stones vanished.
The shadow was not filled it went on growing.
That was one day.

The next day was just the same it went on growing.
They did all the same things it was just the same.
They decided to take its water from under it.
They took away water they took it away the water went down.
The shadow stayed where it was before.
It went on growing it grew onto the land.
They started to scrape the shadow with machines.
When it touched the machines it stayed on them.
They started to beat the shadow with sticks.
Where it touched the sticks it stayed on them.
They started to beat the shadow with hands.
Where it touched the hands it stayed on them.
That was another day.

Well the next day started about the same it went on growing.
They pushed lights into the shadow.
Where the shadow got onto them they went out.
They began to stomp on the edge it got their feet.
And when it got their feet they fell down.
It got into eyes the eyes went blind.
The ones that fell down it grew over and they vanished.
The ones that went blind and walked into it vanished.

The ones that could see and stood still
It swallowed their shadows.
Then it swallowed them too and they vanished.
Well the others ran.

The ones that were left went away to live if it would let them.
They went as far as they could.
The lucky ones with their shadows.

SOME LAST QUESTIONS

What is the head
      a.   Ash
What are the eyes
      a.   The wells have fallen in and have
           Inhabitants
What are the feet
      a.   Thumbs left after the auction
No what are the feet
      a.   Under them the impossible road is moving
           Down which the broken necked mice push
           Balls of blood with their noses
What is the tongue
      a.   The black coat that fell off the wall
           With sleeves trying to say something
What are the hands
      a.   Paid
No what are the hands
      a.   Climbing back down the museum wall
           To their ancestors the extinct shrews that will
           Have left a message
What is the silence
      a.   As though it had a right to more
Who are the compatriots
      a.   They make the stars of bone

WHENEVER I GO THERE

Whenever I go there everything is changed

The stamps on the bandages the titles
Of the professors of water

The portrait of Glare the reasons for
The white mourning

In new rocks new insects are sitting
With the lights off
And once more I remember that the beginning

Is broken

No wonder the addresses are torn

To which I make my way eating the silence of animals
Offering snow to the darkness

Today belongs to few and tomorrow to no one

THE RIVER OF BEES

In a dream I returned to the river of bees
Five orange trees by the bridge and
Beside two mills my house
Into whose courtyard a blind man followed
The goats and stood singing
Of what was older

Soon it will be fifteen years

He was old he will have fallen into his eyes

I took my eyes
A long way to the calendars
Room after room asking how shall I live

One of the ends is made of streets
One man processions carry through it
Empty bottles their
Image of hope
It was offered to me by name

Once once and once
In the same city I was born
Asking what shall I say

He will have fallen into his mouth
Men think they are better than grass

I return to his voice rising like a forkful of hay

He was old he is not real nothing is real
Nor the noise of death drawing water

We are the echo of the future

On the door it says what to do to survive
But we were not born to survive
Only to live

Frank O'Hara

POEM

The eager note on my door said "Call me,
call when you get in!" so I quickly threw
a few tangerines into my overnight bag,
straightened my eyelids and shoulders, and

headed straight for the door. It was autumn
by the time I got around the corner, oh all
unwilling to be either pertinent or bemused, but
the leaves were brighter than grass on the sidewalk!

Funny, I thought, that the lights are on this late
and the hall door open; still up at this hour, a
champion jai-alai player like himself? Oh fie!
for shame! What a host, so zealous! And he was

there in the hall, flat on a sheet of blood that
ran down the stairs. I did appreciate it. There are few
hosts who so thoroughly prepare to greet a guest
only casually invited, and that several months ago.

TO THE HARBORMASTER

I wanted to be sure to reach you;
though my ship was on the way it got caught
in some moorings. I am always tying up
and then deciding to depart. In storms and
at sunset, with the metallic coils of the tide
around my fathomless arms, I am unable

to understand the forms of my vanity
or I am hard alee with my Polish rudder
in my hand and the sun sinking. To
you I offer my hull and the tattered cordage
of my will. The terrible channels where
the wind drives me against the brown lips
of the reeds are not all behind me. Yet
I trust the sanity of my vessel; and
if it sinks, it may well be in answer
to the reasoning of the eternal voices,
the waves which have kept me from reaching you.

ODE TO JOY

We shall have everything we want and there'll be no more dying
        on the pretty plains or in the supper clubs
for our symbol we'll acknowledge vulgar materialistic laughter
        over an insatiable sexual appetite
and the streets will be filled with racing forms
and the photographs of murderers and narcissists and movie stars
        will swell from the walls and books alive in steaming rooms
        to press against our burning flesh not once but interminably
as water flows down hill into the full lipped basin
and the adder dives for the ultimate ostrich egg
and the feather cushion preens beneath a reclining monolith
        that's sweating with post-exertion visibility and sweetness
        near the grave of love
                                        No more dying

We shall see the grave of love as a lovely sight and temporary
        near the elm that spells the lovers' names in roots
and there'll be no more music but the ears in lips and no more
        wit but tongues in ears and no more drums but ears to
        thighs
as evening signals nudities unknown to ancestors' imaginations
and the imagination itself will stagger like a tired paramour of

ivory under the sculptural necessities of lust that never
falters like a six-mile runner from Sweden or Liberia
covered with gold
as lava flows up and over the far-down somnolent city's
abdication
and the hermit always wanting to be lone is lone at last
and the weight of external heat crushes the heat-hating Puritan
who's self-defeating vice becomes a proper sepulchre at last
that love may live

Buildings will go up into the dizzy air as love itself goes in
and up the reeling life that it has chosen for once or all
while in the sky a feeling of intemperate fondness will excite the
birds to swoop and veer like flies crawling across absorbèd
limbs
that weep a pearly perspiration on the sheets of brief attention
and the hairs dry out that summon anxious declaration of the
organs as they rise like buildings to the needs of temporary
neighbors pouring hunger through the heart to feed desire in
intravenous ways
like the ways of gods with humans in the innocent combination of
light
and flesh or as the legends ride their heroes through the dark to
found
great cities where all life is possible to maintain as long as time
which wants us to remain for cocktails in a bar and after
dinner lets us live with it

> No more dying

11/13/57

from *SECOND AVENUE*

5

or are you myself,
indifferent as a drunkard sponging off a car window?
Are you effeminate, like an eyelid, or are you feminine,
like a painting by Picasso? You fled when you followed,

and now the bamboo veils of intemperance are flapping down
with tigerish yaps over the paling corduroy doorway
which was once a capacious volute filled with airplanes,
and that was not a distance, that simple roaring and vagueness.
You are lean, achieved, ravished, acute, light, tan,
waving, stolen, lissome in whispering, salivary in intent,
similar to the sole support of a love affair, so artful,
and loyal only to faults. I found myself equal to every . . .

"Oh the droppings from the trees! the little clam shells,
their bosoms thrust into the clouds and kiss-stained!
I met Joe, his hair pale as the eyes of fields of maize
in August, at the gallery, he said you're the first Creon
of 1953, congrats. Your costume, he said, was hand
over fist. If you worked harder you could remake
old Barrymore movies, you're that statuesque, he said.
For when the window, the ice in it, ran, the fish leaped forth
and returned where they wished to return to and from,
as in a rainbow the end keeps leaping towards the middle
which is the shape of all flowers, and of all flowers
the most exotic." Yes! yes! it was cerulean, oh my darling!
"And the simple yet exquisite pertinence of that race
above the airfield, those tubby little planes flopping
competitively into the wind sleeve, was keen as a violin,
as colorless and as intent. It seemed there was no one there
but children, and at each flaming accident a crumbling giggle
tumbleweeded over the flats and into the hangars and echoed.
What must the fliers have thought? a performance
like a plate of ham and eggs eaten with a fur collar on.
I kept jingling the coins in my pocket and patting
the dollar bills that rustled like so many horses' hooves
against my anxious thigh. He was up there,
the one who ruined my sister while she was still a look
of spiritual withdrawal in my maiden aunt's memories
of bathing at Onset. I always win at Japanese bowling.
I won a piano with a flowered shawl draped over it
and a photograph of Anna Sten beside a trembling yellow vase."

Screaming and tearing at her breasts she bent over,

terribly pale and yet trifling with her feelings before him,
the heavy bronze crucifix he had stepped on, quite
accidentally, mistaking it for a moth, tinea pellionella
which, in its labors against death, another more
vibrantly mournful kind, renders mankind subtly naked;
more than her eyes could stand, she went bloated into the azure
like a shot. Greying even more steadily now he remembered
the afternoon game of marbles beside the firehouse
and how the scum settled on his shoulders as he swam
and the many tasks done and forgotten and famous which,
as a pilot, he had disdained, trusting to luck always.
"Arabella" was the word he had muttered that moment
when lightning had smelled sweet over the zoo of the waves
while he played on and on and on and the women grew hysterical.
Of heldness and of caresses you have become the entrepreneur.
The sea looked like so many amethyst prophets and I,
hadn't the cannery sent forth perfume? would never go back.
And then staggering forward into the astounding capaciousness
of his own rumor he became violent as an auction,
rubbed the hairs on his chest with bottles of snarling
and deared the frying pan that curtained the windows
with his tears. I remember I felt at that moment the elephant
kissing. When paralysis becomes jaundice and jaundice
is blushing, a linen map of ecstasy hangs next the range
where the peas are burning and memories of Swan Lake
aspire like Victoria Falls to a jacket of dust.

You are too young to remember the lack of snow in 1953 showing:
"1   Except that you react like electricity to a chunk of cloth,
it will disappear like an ape at night. 2   Before eating
there was a closing of retina against retina, and ice,
telephone wires! was knotted, spelling out farce
which is germane to lust. 3   Then the historic duel in the surf
when black garments were wasted and swept over battlements
into the moat. 4   The book contained a rosary pressed
in the shape of a tongue. 5   The hill had begun to roll
luminously. A deck appeared among the fir trees, Larry's
uncle sent a missionary to India when he was in grade school
who cried 'Go straight' to the white men there. Forgiveness

)f heat. 6   Green lips pressed his body like a pearl shell.
7   It all took place in darkness, and meant more earlier
when they were in different places and didn't know each other.
As is often misprinted." And such whiteness not there!
All right, all right, all right, you glass of coke, empty
your exceptionally neonish newspaper from such left hands
with headlines to be grey as cut WITHER ACCEPTED AS
       SELLING.
(The western mountain ranges were sneaking along "Who
taps wires and why?" like a pack of dogies and is there much
tapping under the desert moon? Does it look magical
or realistic, that landing? And the riverboat put in there,
keeps putting in, with all the slaves' golden teeth and arms,
selfconscious without their weapons. Joe LeSueur,
the handsome Captain who smuggles Paris perfumes, tied up
at the arroyo and with thunderous hooves swam across a causeway
to make the Honest Dollar. In Pasadena they are calling
"Higho, Silver!" but in the High Sierras they just shoot
movie after movie. Who is "they"? The Westerners, of course,
the tans. Didn't you ever want to be a cowboy, buster?) Big-
town papers, you see, and this great-coated tour of the teens
n (oh bless me!) imagination. That's what the snow said,
"and doesn't your penis look funny today?" I jacked "off".

POEM EN FORME DE SAW

I ducked out of sight behind the saw-mill
nobody saw me because of the falls the gates the sluice the tourist
                                                              boats
the children were trailing their fingers in the water
and the swans, regal and smarty, were nipping their "little" fingers
I heard one swan remark "That was a good nip
though they are not as interesting as sausages" and another
reply "Nor as tasty as those peasants we got away from the
                                          elephant that time"
but I didn't really care for conversation that day
I wanted to be alone

which is why I went to the mill in the first place
now I am alone and hate it
I don't want to just make boards for the rest of my life
I'm distressed
the water is very beautiful but you can't go into it
because of the gunk
and the dog is always rolling over, I like dogs on their "little" fee
I think I may scamper off to Winnipeg to see Raymond
but what'll happen to the mill
I see the cobwebs collecting already
and later those other webs, those awful predatory webs
if I stay right here I will eventually get into the newspapers
like Robert Frost
willow trees, willow trees they remind me of Desdemona
I'm so damned literary
and at the same time the waters rushing past remind me of nothing
I'm so damned empty
what is all this vessel shit anyway
we are all rushing down the River Happy Times
ducking poling bumping sinking and swimming
and we arrive at the beach
the chaff is sand
alone as a tree bumping another tree in a storm
that's not really being alone, is it, signed The Saw

Sylvia Plath

THE BEE MEETING

Who are these people at the bridge to meet me? They are the
    villagers——
The rector, the midwife, the sexton, the agent for bees.
In my sleeveless summery dress I have no protection,
And they are all gloved and covered, why did nobody tell me?
They are smiling and taking out veils tacked to ancient hats.

I am nude as a chicken neck, does nobody love me?
Yes, here is the secretary of bees with her white shop smock,
Buttoning the cuffs at my wrists and the slit from my neck to my
    knees.
Now I am milkweed silk, the bees will not notice.
They will not smell my fear, my fear, my fear.

Which is the rector now, is it that man in black?
Which is the midwife, is that her blue coat?
Everybody is nodding a square black head, they are knights in visors,
Breastplates of cheesecloth knotted under the armpits.
Their smiles and their voices are changing. I am led through a bean-
    field.

Strips of tinfoil winking like people,
Feather dusters fanning their hands in a sea of bean flowers,
Creamy bean flowers with black eyes and leaves like bored hearts.
Is it blood clots the tendrils are dragging up that string?
No, no, it is scarlet flowers that will one day be edible.

Now they are giving me a fashionable white straw Italian hat
And a black veil that moulds to my face, they are making me one
    of them.
They are leading me to the shorn grove, the circle of hives.

Is it the hawthorn that smells so sick?
The barren body of hawthorn, etherizing its children.

Is it some operation that is taking place?
It is the surgeon my neighbours are waiting for,
This apparition in a green helmet,
Shining gloves and white suit.
Is it the butcher, the grocer, the postman, someone I know?

I cannot run, I am rooted, and the gorse hurts me
With its yellow purses, its spiky armoury.
I could not run without having to run forever.
The white hive is snug as a virgin,
Sealing off her brood cells, her honey, and quietly humming.

Smoke rolls and scarves in the grove.
The mind of the hive thinks this is the end of everything.
Here they come, the outriders, on their hysterical elastics.
If I stand very still, they will think I am cow parsley,
A gullible head untouched by their animosity,

Not even nodding, a personage in a hedgerow.
The villagers open the chambers, they are hunting the queen.
Is she hiding, is she eating honey? She is very clever.
She is old, old, old, she must live another year, and she knows it.
While in their fingerjoint cells the new virgins

Dream of a duel they will win inevitably,
A curtain of wax dividing them from the bride flight,
The upflight of the murderess into a heaven that loves her.
The villagers are moving the virgins, there will be no killing.
The old queen does not show herself, is she so ungrateful?

I am exhausted, I am exhausted——
Pillar of white in a blackout of knives.
I am the magician's girl who does not flinch.
The villagers are untying their disguises, they are shaking hands.
Whose is that long white box in the grove, what have they accomplished, why am I cold?

THE ARRIVAL OF THE BEE BOX

I ordered this, this clean wood box
Square as a chair and almost too heavy to lift.
I would say it was the coffin of a midget
Or a square baby
Were there not such a din in it.

The box is locked, it is dangerous.
I have to live with it overnight
And I can't keep away from it.
There are no windows, so I can't see what is in there.
There is only a little grid, no exit.

I put my eye to the grid.
It is dark, dark,
With the swarmy feeling of African hands
Minute and shrunk for export,
Black on black, angrily clambering.

How can I let them out?
It is the noise that appals me most of all,
The unintelligible syllables.
It is like a Roman mob,
Small, taken one by one, but my god, together!

I lay my ear to furious Latin.
I am not a Caesar.
I have simply ordered a box of maniacs.
They can be sent back.
They can die, I need feed them nothing, I am the owner.

I wonder how hungry they are.
I wonder if they would forget me
If I just undid the locks and stood back and turned into a tree.
There is the laburnum, its blond colonnades,
And the petticoats of the cherry.

They might ignore me immediately
In my moon suit and funeral veil.
I am no source of honey
So why should they turn on me?
Tomorrow I will be sweet God, I will set them free.

The box is only temporary.

THE NIGHT DANCES

A smile fell in the grass.
Irretrievable!

And how will your night dances
Lose themselves. In mathematics?

Such pure leaps and spirals——
Surely they travel

The world forever, I shall not entirely
Sit emptied of beauties, the gift

Of your small breath, the drenched grass
Smell of your sleeps, lilies, lilies.

Their flesh bears no relation.
Cold folds of ego, the calla,

And the tiger, embellishing itself——
Spots, and a spread of hot petals.

The comets
Have such a space to cross,

Such coldness, forgetfulness.
So your gestures flake off——

Warm and human, then their pink light
Bleeding and peeling

Through the black amnesias of heaven.
Why am I given

These lamps, these planets
Falling like blessings, like flakes

Six-sided, white
On my eyes, my lips, my hair

Touching and melting.
Nowhere.

DEATH & CO.

Two, of course there are two.
It seems perfectly natural now——
The one who never looks up, whose eyes are lidded
And balled, like Blake's,
Who exhibits

The birthmarks that are his trademark——
The scald scar of water,
The nude
Verdigris of the condor.
I am red meat. His beak

Claps sidewise: I am not his yet.
He tells me how badly I photograph.
He tells me how sweet
The babies look in their hospital
Icebox, a simple

Frill at the neck,
Then the flutings of their Ionian

Death-gowns,
Then two little feet.
He does not smile or smoke.

The other does that,
His hair long and plausive.
Bastard
Masturbating a glitter,
He wants to be loved.

I do not stir.
The frost makes a flower,
The dew makes a star,
The dead bell,
The dead bell.

Somebody's done for.

Adrienne Rich

LIVING IN SIN

She had thought the studio would keep itself;
no dust upon the furniture of love.
Half heresy, to wish the taps less vocal,
the panes relieved of grime. A plate of pears,
a piano with a Persian shawl, a cat
stalking the picturesque amusing mouse
had risen at his urging.
Not that at five each separate stair would writhe
under the milkman's tramp; that morning light
so coldly would delineate the scraps
of last night's cheese and three sepulchral bottles;
that on the kitchen shelf among the saucers
a pair of beetle-eyes would fix her own—
envoy from some black village in the mouldings . . .
Meanwhile, he, with a yawn,
sounded a dozen notes upon the keyboard,
declared it out of tune, shrugged at the mirror,
rubbed at his beard, went out for cigarettes;
while she, jeered by the minor demons,
pulled back the sheets and made the bed and found
a towel to dust the table-top,
and let the coffee-pot boil over on the stove.
By evening she was back in love again,
though not so wholly but throughout the night
she woke sometimes to feel the daylight coming
like a relentless milkman up the stairs.

THE ROOFWALKER

for Denise Levertov

Over the half-finished houses
night comes. The builders
stand on the roof. It is
quiet after the hammers,
the pulleys hang slack.
Giants, the roofwalkers,
on a listing deck, the wave
of darkness about to break
on their heads. The sky
is a torn sail where figures
pass magnified, shadows
on a burning deck.

I feel like them up there:
exposed, larger than life,
and due to break my neck.

Was it worth while to lay—
with infinite exertion—
a roof I can't live under?
—All those blueprints,
closings of gaps,
measurings, calculations?
A life I didn't choose
chose me: even
my tools are the wrong ones
for what I have to do.
I'm naked, ignorant,
a naked man fleeing
across the roofs
who could with a shade of difference
be sitting in the lamplight
against the cream wallpaper

reading—not with indifference—
about a naked man
fleeing across the roofs.

THE AFTERWAKE

Nursing your nerves
to rest, I've roused my own; well,
now for a few bad hours!
Sleep sees you behind closed doors.
Alone, I slump in his front parlor.
You're safe inside. Good. But I'm
like a midwife who at dawn
has all in order: bloodstains
washed up, teapot on the stove,
and starts her five miles home
walking, the birthyell still
exploding in her head.

Yes, I'm with her now: here's
the streaked, livid road
edged with shut houses
breathing night out and in.
Legs tight with fatigue,
we move under morning's coal-blue star,
colossal as this load
of unexpired purpose, which drains
slowly, till scissors of cockcrow snip the air.

JUVENILIA

Your Ibsen volumes, violet-spined,
each flaking its gold arabesque!
Again I sit, under duress, hands washed,
at your inkstained oaken desk,

by the goose-neck lamp in the tropic of your books,
stabbing the blotting-pad, doodling loop upon loop,
peering one-eyed in the dusty reflecting mirror
of your student microscope,
craning my neck to spell above me

A DOLLS HOUSE   LITTLE EYOLF
        WHEN WE DEAD AWAKEN

Unspeakable fairy tales ebb like blood through my head
as I dip the pen and for aunts, for admiring friends,
for you above all to read,
copy my praised and sedulous lines.

Behind the two of us, thirsty spines
quiver in semi-shadow, huge leaves uncurl and thicken.

RURAL REFLECTIONS

This is the grass your feet are planted on.
You paint it orange or you sing it green,
        But you have never found
A way to make the grass mean what you mean.

A cloud can be whatever you intend:
Ostrich or leaning tower or staring eye.
        But you have never found
A cloud sufficient to express the sky.

Get out there with your splendid expertise;
Raymond who cuts the meadow does no less.
        Inhuman nature says:
Inhuman patience is the true success.

Human impatience trips you as you run;
        Stand still and you must lie.
It is the grass that cuts the mower down;
It is the cloud that swallows up the sky.

PEELING ONIONS

Only to have a grief
equal to all these tears!

There's not a sob in my chest.
Dry-hearted as Peer Gynt
I pare away, no hero,
merely a cook.

Crying was labor, once
when I'd good cause.
Walking, I felt my eyes like wounds
raw in my head,
so postal-clerks, I thought, must stare.
A dog's look, a cat's, burnt to my brain—
yet all that stayed
stuffed in my lungs like smog.

These old tears in the chopping-bowl.

IN THE WOODS

"Difficult ordinary happiness,"
no one nowadays believes in you.
I shift, full-length on the blanket,
to fix the sun precisely

behind the pine-tree's crest
so light spreads through the needles
alive as water just
where a snake has surfaced,

unreal as water in green crystal.
Bad news is always arriving.

"We're hiders, hiding from something bad,"
sings the little boy.

Writing these words in the woods,
I feel like a traitor to my friends,
even to my enemies.
The common lot's to die

a stranger's death and lie
rouged in the coffin, in a dress
chosen by the funeral director.
Perhaps that's why we never

see clocks on public buildings any more.
A fact no architect will mention.
We're hiders, hiding from something bad
most of the time.

Yet, and outrageously, something good
finds us, found me this morning
lying on a dusty blanket
among the burnt-out Indian pipes

and bursting-open lady's-slippers.
My soul, my helicopter, whirred
distantly, by habit, over
the old pond with the half-drowned boat

toward which it always veers
for consolation: ego's Arcady:
leaving the body stuck
like a leaf against a screen.—

Happiness! how many times
I've stranded on that word,
at the edge of that pond; seen
as if through tears, the dragon-fly—

only to find it all

going differently for once
this time: my soul wheeled back
and burst into my body.

Found! ready or not.
If I move now, the sun
naked between the trees
will melt me as I lie.

THE TREES

The trees inside are moving out into the forest,
the forest that was empty all these days
where no bird could sit
no insect hide
no sun bury its feet in shadow
the forest that was empty all these nights
will be full of trees by morning.

All night the roots work
to disengage themselves from the cracks
in the veranda floor.
The leaves strain toward the glass
small twigs stiff with exertion
long-cramped boughs shuffling under the roof
like newly discharged patients
half-dazed, moving
to the clinic doors.

I sit inside, doors open to the veranda
writing long letters
in which I scarcely mention the departure
of the forest from the house.
The night is fresh, the whole moon shines
in a sky still open
the smell of leaves and lichen
still reaches like a voice into the rooms.

My head is full of whispers
which tomorrow will be silent.

Listen. The glass is breaking.
The trees are stumbling forward
into the night. Winds rush to meet them.
The moon is broken like a mirror,
its pieces flash now in the crown
of the tallest oak.

LIKE THIS TOGETHER

for A.H.C.

1

Wind rocks the car.
We sit parked by the river,
silence between our teeth.
Birds scatter across islands
of broken ice. Another time
I'd have said "Canada geese,"
knowing you love them.
A year, ten years from now
I'll remember this—
this sitting like drugged birds
in a glass case—
not why, only that we
were here like this together.

2

They're tearing down, tearing up
this city, block by block.
Rooms cut in half
hang like flayed carcasses,
their old roses in rags,

famous streets have forgotten
where they were going. Only
a fact could be so dreamlike.
They're tearing down the houses
we met and lived in,
soon our two bodies will be all
left standing from that era.

3

We have, as they say,
certain things in common.
I mean: a view
over slate to stiff pigeons
huddled every morning; the way
water tastes from our tap,
which you marvel at, letting
it splash into the glass.
Because of you I notice
the taste of water,
a luxury I might
otherwise have missed.

4

Our words misunderstand us.
Sometimes at night
you are my mother:
old detailed griefs
twitch at my dreams, and I
crawl against you, fighting
for shelter, making you
my cave. Sometimes
you're the wave of birth
that drowns me in my first
nightmare. I suck the air.
Miscarried knowledge twists us
like hot sheets thrown askew.

5

Dead winter doesn't die,
it wears away, a piece of carrion
picked clean at last,
rained away or burnt dry.
Our desiring does this,
make no mistake, I'm speaking
of fact: through mere indifference
we could prevent it.
Only our fierce attention
gets hyacinths out of those
hard cerebral lumps,
unwraps the wet buds down
the whole length of a stem.

TWO SONGS

1

Sex, as they harshly call it,
I fell into this morning
at ten o'clock, a drizzling hour
of traffic and wet newspapers.
I thought of him who yesterday
clearly didn't
turn me to a hot field
ready for plowing,
and longing for that young man
pierced me to the roots
bathing every vein, etc.
All day he appears to me
touchingly desirable,
a prize one could wreck one's peace for.
I'd call it love if love
didn't take so many years
but lust too is a jewel

a sweet flower and what
pure happiness to know
all our high-toned questions
breed in a lively animal.

2

That "old last act"!
And yet sometimes
all seems post coitum triste
and I a mere bystander.
Somebody else is going off,
getting shot to the moon.
Or, a moon-race!
Split seconds after
my opposite number lands
I make it—
we lie fainting together
at a crater-edge
heavy as mercury in our moonsuits
till he speaks—
in a different language
yet one I've picked up
through cultural exchanges . . .
we murmur the first moonwords:
Spasibo. Thanks. O.K.

Frederick Seidel

WANTING TO LIVE IN HARLEM

Pictures of violins in the Wurlitzer collection
Were my bedroom's one decoration,
Besides a blue horse and childish tan maiden by Gauguin—
Backs, bellies and scrolls,
Stradivarius, Guarnerius, Amati,
Colored like a calabash-and-meerschaum pipe bowl's
Warmed, matured body—

The color of the young light-skinned colored girl we had then.
I used to dream about her often,
In sheets she'd have to change the day after.
I was thirteen, had just been bar mitzvah.
My hero, once I'd read about him,
Was the Emperor Hadrian; my villain, Bar Kochba,
The Jew Hadrian had crushed out at Jerusalem:

Both in the *Cambridge Ancient History's* Hadrian chapter (1936
Edition), by some German. (The Olympics
Year of my birth and Jesse Owens' *putsch* it had appeared.)
Even then, in '49, my mother was dying.
Dressed in her fresh-air blue starched uniform,
The maid would come from mother's room crying
With my mother's tears shining on her arm,

And run to grab her beads and crucifix and missal,
I to find my violin and tuning whistle
To practice my lessons. Mendelssohn. Or Bach,
Whose Lutheran fingering had helped pluck
The tonsured monks like toadstools from their lawns,
And now riddled the armor I would have to shuck:
His were life-sized hands behind his puppet Mendelssohn's.

One night, by the blue of her nitelite, I watched the maid
Weaving before her mirror in the dark, naked.
Her eyes rolled, whiskey-bright; the glass was black, dead.
"Will you come true? It's me, it's me," she said.
Her hands and her hips clung to her rolling pelvis.
Her lips smacked and I saw her smile, pure lead
And silver, like a child, and shape a kiss.

All night I tossed. I saw the face,
The shoulders and the slight breasts—but a boy's face,
A soft thing tangled, singing, in his arms,
Singing and foaming, while his blinding pelvis,
Scooped out, streamed. His white eyes dreamed,
While the black face pounded with syncope and madness.
And then, in clear soprano, we both screamed.

What a world of mirrored darkness! Agonized, elated,
Again years later I would see it with my naked
Eye—see Harlem: doped up and heartless,
Loved up by heroin, running out of veins
And out of money and out of arms to hold it—where
I saw dead saplings wired to stakes in lanes
Of ice, like hair out cold in hair straightener.

And that wintry morning, trudging through Harlem
Looking for furnished rooms, I heard the solemn
Pedal-toned bowing of the Bach Chaconne.
I'd played it once! How many tears
Had shined on mother's maids since then?
Ten years! I had been trying to find a room ten years,
It seemed that day, and been turned down again and again.

No violin could thaw
The rickety and raw
Purple window I shivered below, stamping my shoes.
Two boys in galoshes came goosestepping down
The sheer-ice long white center line of Lenox Avenue.
A blue-stormcoated Negro patrolman,
With a yellowing badge star, bawled at them. I left too.

I had given up violin and left St. Louis,
I had given up being Jewish,
To be at Harvard just another
Greek nose in street clothes in Harvard Yard.
Mother went on half dying.
I wanted to live in Harlem. I was almost unarmored . . .
Almost alone—like Hadrian crying

As his death came on, "Your Hadrianus
Misses you, Antinous,
Misses your ankles slender as your wrists,
Dear child. We want to be alone.
His back was the city gates of Rome.
And now Jerusalem is dust in the sun,
His skies are blue. He's coming, child, I come."

David Shapiro

THE WILL

1

I know the party of the sun
The sun dirigent and wealthy over the hair
The sun of round cancer on the gray breasts of the sky

and I understand that the commitment of the intellect is pitiful
even in the stage of the lapse of mind, where the speech is senseless
and the jaw kind and calm as a child's mouth.

Then fathers moping in the stove of the sun
grieve all their school and tears of a will
that drove them so, the intellect and changes of the Sun.

But when the jaw falls, and the stars are perfect depressions
in the sky thru which the wind dwindles and thru the stiff oak branches
I can see the advantage of literature to the mind.

And, at last, I become serious, in this room, with a smile.
And the directions of the wind and sun outside this room
remind me

of where the brown fields, in the wind, and the park
become silent; and I notice also, distinctly and quietly, in this room,
the insinuations of men turning to their wives in the descending cars.

2

That fit of one heart is a predicament. But what arrives, what
arrives like the monk of the flesh? Who is that gaping guest

rules in the kingless blood and makes us men?
I hear the paltry wind bang at the homely boughs

and the highways of men turn to their wives under the moon.
What rings the sky in the cloud, what drives the sea?
What visible hero and what dark face of this woman
who takes her hands from her cheeks and holds the infant up

to tears, in the night, as the ragged boys congratulate and borrow
from the heart of the lady holding the infant in her wellbeing
and the screams of the infant born again and again
in the dark to every citizen of a name.

3

When shall we wake to the recession of dreams?
Is it to wish the rose the profit of the loam
or the August star the ethic of the sky?
Tonight the children wish they had made friends.

And those weapons which separate us from the sun
and from each other, the will shall keep
from all imagining,
born of an outburst and cudgeling light.

So that all who survived the mind of a man are
wealthy men, who are defended and understood;
and those who grip an hour of blood within their hands
—and die of Silence in the year of reasonable men.

FIRST LOVE

I imagine you dressed up as a gowned Hasid
A blackbearded girl—a girl I might have married
A stick we take to bed and call John in bed
Later a white-breasted Protestant girl to be buried.
Who are you and what cruelty in what theater

Do you still play cello and strip for friends
Atlantic City fingers warmed by the electric-heater
Sun—a decadent image everybody understands.

And you smile by the chorus of a Psalm of David
Your smile twirls in the air just before I cry
"Your team is my team" and you change the bid
On your body to a strangulating price I cannot buy.
Slowly walking in Boston with a music note
Your composition stabs me like a bat.

Jon Silkin

DEATH OF A SON

(who died in a mental hospital aged one)

Something has ceased to come along with me.
Something like a person: something very like one.
  And there was no nobility in it
    Or anything like that.

Something was there like a one year
Old house, dumb as stone. While the near buildings
  Sang like birds and laughed
    Understanding the pact

They were to have with silence. But he
Neither sang nor laughed. He did not bless silence
  Like bread, with words.
    He did not forsake silence.

But rather, like a house in mourning
Kept the eye turned in to watch the silence while
  The other houses like birds
    Sang around him.

And the breathing silence neither
Moved nor was still.

I have seen stones: I have seen brick
But this house was made up of neither bricks nor stone
  But a house of flesh and blood
    With flesh of stone

And bricks for blood. A house

Of stones and blood in breathing silence with the other
      Birds singing crazy on its chimneys.
         But this was silence,

    This was something else, this was
Hearing and speaking though he was a house drawn
      Into silence, this was
         Something religious in his silence,

    Something shining in his quiet,
This was different this was altogether something else:
      Though he never spoke, this
         Was something to do with death.

    And then slowly the eye stopped looking
Inward. The silence rose and became still.
The look turned to the outer place and stopped,
      With the birds still shrilling around him.
        And as if he could speak

He turned over on his side with his one year
Red as a wound
He turned over as if he could be sorry for this
And out of his eyes two great tears rolled, like stones,
      and he died.

CARING FOR ANIMALS

I ask sometimes why these small animals
With bitter eyes, why we should care for them.

I question the sky, the serene blue water,
But it cannot say. It gives no answer.

And no answer releases in my head
A procession of grey shades patched and whimpering.

Dogs with clipped ears, wheezing cart horses
A fly without shadow and without thought.

Is it with these menaces to our vision
With this procession led by a man carrying wood

We must be concerned? The holy land, the rearing
Green island should be kindlier than this.

Yet the animals, our ghosts, need tending to.
Take in the whipped cat and the blinded owl;

Take up the man-trapped squirrel upon your shoulder.
Attend to the unnecessary beasts.

From growing mercy and a moderate love
Great love for the human animal occurs.

And your love grows. Your great love grows and grows.

FURNISHED LIVES

I have been walking today
Where the sour children of London's poor sleep
    Pressed close to the unfrosted glare,
Torment lying closed in tenement,
    Of the clay fire; I
Have watched their whispering souls fly straight to God:

    "O Lord, please give to us
A dinner-service, austere, yet gay: like snow
    When swans are on it; Bird,
Unfold your wings until like a white smile
    You fill this mid-white room."
I have balanced myself on the meagre Strand where

Each man and woman turn,
On the deliberate hour of the cock
        As if two new risen souls,
Through the cragged landscape in each other's eyes.
        But where lover upon lover
Should meet—where sheet, and pillow, and eiderdown

        Should frolic, and crisp,
As dolphins on the stylized crown of the sea
        Their pale cerements lie.
They tread with chocolate souls and paper hands;
        They walk into that room
Your gay and daffodil smile has never seen;

        Not to love's pleasant feast
They go, in the mutations of the night,
        But to their humiliations
Paled as a swan's dead feather scorched in the sun.
        I have been walking today
Among the newly paper-crowned, among those

        Whose casual, paper body
Is crushed between fate's fingers and the platter;
        But Sir, their perpetual fire
Was not stubbed out, folded on brass or stone
        Extinguished in the dark,
But burns with the drear dampness of cut flowers.

        I cannot hear their piped
Cry. These souls have no players. They have resigned
        The vivid performance of their world.
                And your world, Lord,
                    Has now become
Like a dumb winter show, held in one room,

        Which must now reek of age
Before you have retouched its lips with such straight fire
        As through your stony earth

Burns with ferocious tears in the world's eyes:
Church-stone, door-knocker, and polished railway lines
    Move in their separate dumb way
       So why not these lives:
I ask you often, but you never say?

THE COLDNESS

Where the printing-works buttress a church
And the northern river like moss
Robes herself slowly through
The cold township of York,
More slowly than usual
For a cold, northern river,
You see the citizens
Indulging stately pleasures,
Like swans. But they seem cold.
Why have they been so punished:
In what do their sins consist now?
An assertion persistent
As a gross tumour, and the sense
Of such growth haunting
The flesh of York
Is that there has been
No synagogue since eleven ninety
When eight hundred Jews
Took each other's lives
To escape christian death
By christian hand; and the last
Took his own. The event
Has the frigid persistence of a growth
In the flesh. It is a fact
No other fact can be added to
Save that it was Easter, the time
When the dead christian God

Rose again. It is in this,
Perhaps, they are haunted; for the cold
Blood of victims is colder,
More staining, more corrosive
On the soul, than the blood of martyrs.
What consciousness is there of the cold
Heart, with its spaces?
For nothing penetrates
More than admitted absence.
The heart in warmth, even, cannot
Close its gaps. Absence of Jews
Through hatred, or indifference,
A gap they slip through, a conscience
That corrodes more deeply since it is
Forgotten — this deadens York.
Where are the stone-masons, the builders
Skilled in glass, strong first in wood:
Taut, flaxen plumbers with lengths of pipe,
Steel rules coiled in their palms;
The printers; canopy-makers —
Makers in the institution of marriage?
Their absence is endless, a socket
Where the jaw is protected neither
Through its tolerance for tooth,
Nor for blood. Either there is pain or no pain.
If they could feel; were there one
Among them with this kind
Of sensitivity that
Could touch the dignity,
Masonry of the cold
Northern face that falls
As you touch it, there might
Be some moving to
A northern expurgation.
All Europe is touched
With some of frigid York,
As York is now by Europe.

THE CHILD

Something that can be heard
Is a grasping of soft fingers
Behind that door.
Oh come in, please come in
And be seated.

It was hard to be sure,
Because for some time a creature
Had bitten at the wood.
But this was something else; a pure noise
Humanly shaped

That gently insists on
Being present. I am sure you are.
Look: the pots over the fire
On a shelf, just put;
So, and no other way,

Are as you have seen them; and you,
Being visible, make them no different.
No man nor thing shall take
Your place from you; so little,
You would think, to ask for.

I have not denied; you know that.
Do you? Do you see
How you are guttered
At a breath, a flicker from me?
Burn more then.

Move this way with me,
Over the stone. Here are
Your father's utensils on
The kitchen wall; cling
As I lead you.

It seems you have come without speech,
And flesh. If it be love
That moves with smallness through
These rooms, speak to me,
As you move.

You have not come with
Me, but burn on the stone.

If I could pick you up
If I could lift you;
Can a thing be weightless?
I have seen, when I did lift you

How your flesh was casually
Pressed in. You have come
Without bone, or blood.
Is that to be preferred?
A flesh without

Sinew, a bone that has
No hardness, and will not snap.
Hair with no spring; without
Juices, touching, or speech.
What are you?

Or rather, show me, since
You cannot speak, that you are real;
A proper effusion of air,
Not that I doubt, blown by a breath
Into my child;

As if you might grow on that vapour
To thought, or natural movement
That expresses, 'I know where I am.'
Yet that you are here,
I feel.

Though you are different.

The brain being touched lightly,
It was gone. Yet since you live,
As if you were not born,
Strangeness of strangeness, speak.

Or rather, touch my breath
With your breath, steadily
And breathe yourself into me.

The soft huge pulsing comes
And passes through my flesh
Out of my hearing.

A DAISY

Look unoriginal
Being numerous. They ask for attention
With that gradated yellow swelling
Of oily stamens. Petals focus them:
The eye-lashes grow wide.
Why should not one bring these to a funeral?
And at night, like children,
Without anxiety, their consciousness
Shut with white petals.

Blithe, individual.

The unwearying, small sunflower
Fills the grass
With versions of one eye.
A strength in the full look
Candid, solid, glad.
Domestic as milk.

In multitudes, wait,
Each, to be looked at, spoken to.
They do not wither;

Their going, a pressure
Of elate sympathy
Released from you.
Rich up to the last interval
With minute tubes of oil, pollen;
Utterly without scent, for the eye,
For the eye, simply. For the mind
And its invisible organ,
That feeling thing.

Louis Simpson

EARLY IN THE MORNING

Early in the morning
The dark Queen said,
"The trumpets are warning
There's trouble ahead."
Spent with carousing,
With wine-soaked wits,
Antony drowsing
Whispered, "It's
Too cold a morning
To get out of bed."

The army's retreating,
The fleet has fled,
Caesar is beating
His drums through the dead.
"Antony, horses!
We'll get away,
Gather our forces
For another day . . ."
"It's a cold morning,"
Antony said.

Caesar Augustus
Cleared his phlegm.
"Corpses disgust us.
Cover them."
Caesar Augustus
In his time lay
Dying, and just as

Cold as they,
On the cold morning
Of a cold day.

THE MAN WHO MARRIED MAGDALENE

The man who married Magdalene
Had not forgiven her.
God might pardon every sin . . .
Love is no pardoner.

Her hands were hollow, pale and blue,
Her mouth like watered wine.
He watched to see if she were true
And waited for a sign.

It was old harlotry, he guessed,
That drained her strength away,
So gladly for the dark she dressed,
So sadly for the day.

Their quarrels made her dull and weak
And soon a man might fit
A penny in the hollow cheek
And never notice it.

At last, as they exhausted slept,
Death granted the divorce,
And nakedly the woman leapt
Upon that narrow horse.

But when he woke and woke alone
He wept and would deny
The loose behavior of the bone
And the immodest thigh.

SUMMER STORM

In that so sudden summer storm they tried
Each bed, couch, closet, carpet, car-seat, table,
Both river banks, five fields, a mountain side,
Covering as much ground as they were able.

A lady, coming on them in the dark
In a white fixture, wrote to the newspapers
Complaining of the statues in the park.
By Cupid, but they cut some pretty capers!

The envious oxen in still rings would stand
Ruminating. Their sweet incessant plows
I think had changed the contours of the land
And made two modest conies move their house.

God rest them well, and firmly shut the door.
Now they are married Nature breathes once more.

MY FATHER IN THE NIGHT
COMMANDING NO

My father in the night commanding No
Has work to do. Smoke issues from his lips;
    He reads in silence.
The frogs are croaking and the streetlamps glow.

And then my mother winds the gramophone;
The Bride of Lammermoor begins to shriek—
    Or reads a story
About a prince, a castle, and a dragon.

The moon is glittering above the hill.

I stand before the gateposts of the King—
      So runs the story—
Of Thule, at midnight when the mice are still.

And I have been in Thule! It has come true—
The journey and the danger of the world,
      All that there is
To bear and to enjoy, endure and do.

Landscapes, seascapes . . . where have I been led?
The names of cities—Paris, Venice, Rome—
      Held out their arms.
A feathered god, seductive, went ahead.

Here is my house. Under a red rose tree
A child is swinging; another gravely plays.
      They are not surprised
That I am here; they were expecting me.

And yet my father sits and reads in silence,
My mother sheds a tear, the moon is still,
      And the dark wind
Is murmuring that nothing ever happens.

Beyond his jurisdiction as I move
Do I not prove him wrong? And yet, it's true
      They will not change
There, on the stage of terror and of love.

The actors in that playhouse always sit
In fixed positions—father, mother, child
      With painted eyes.
How sad it is to be a little puppet!

Their heads are wooden. And you once pretended
To understand them! Shake them as you will,
      They cannot speak.
Do what you will, the comedy is ended.

Father, why did you work? Why did you weep,
Mother? Was the story so important?
    "Listen!" the wind
Said to the children, and they fell asleep.

LINES WRITTEN NEAR SAN FRANCISCO

I wake and feel the city trembling.
Yes, there is something unsettled in the air
And the earth is uncertain.

And so it was for the tenor Caruso.
He couldn't sleep—you know how the ovation
Rings in your ears, and you re-sing your part.

And then the ceiling trembled
And the floor moved. He ran into the street.
Never had Naples given him such a reception!

The air was darker than Vesuvius.
"O mamma mia,"
He cried, "I've lost my voice!"

At that moment the hideous voice of Culture,
Hysterical woman, thrashing her arms and legs,
Shrieked from the ruins.

At that moment everyone became a performer.
Otello and Don Giovanni
And Figaro strode on the midmost stage.

In the high window of a burning castle
Lucia raved. Black horses
Plunged through fire, dragging the wild bells.

The curtains were wrapped in smoke. Tin swords

Were melting; masks and ruffs
Burned—and the costumes of the peasants' chorus.

Night fell. The white moon rose
And sank in the Pacific. The tremors
Passed under the waves. And Death rested.

2

Now, as we stand idle,
Watching the silent, bowler-hatted man,
The engineer, who writes in the smoking field;

Now as he hands the paper to a boy,
Who takes it and runs to a group of waiting men,
And they disperse and move toward their wagons,

Mules bray and the wagons move—
Wait! Before you start
(Already the wheels are rattling on the stones)

Say, did your fathers cross the dry Sierras
To build another London?
Do Americans always have to be second-rate?

Wait! For there are spirits
In the earth itself, or the air, or sea.
Where are the aboriginal American devils?

Cloud shadows, pine shadows
Falling across the bright Pacific bay . . .
(Already they have nailed rough boards together)

Wait only for the wind
That rustles in the eucalyptus tree.
Wait only for the light

That trembles on the petals of a rose.

(The mortar sets—banks are the first to stand)
Wait for a rose, and you may wait forever.

The silent man mops his head and drinks
Cold lemonade. "San Francisco
Is a city second only to Paris."

3

Every night, at the end of America
We taste our wine, looking at the Pacific.
How sad it is, the end of America!

While we were waiting for the land
They'd finished it—with gas drums
On the hilltops, cheap housing in the valleys

Where lives are mean and wretched.
But the banks thrive and the realtors
Rejoice—they have their America.

Still, there is something unsettled in the air.
Out there on the Pacific
There's no America but the Marines.

Whitman was wrong about the People,
But right about himself. The land is within.
At the end of the open road we come to ourselves.

Though mad Columbus follows the sun
Into the sea, we cannot follow.
We must remain, to serve the returning sun,

And to set tables for death.
For we are the colonists of Death—
Not, as some think, of the English.

And we are preparing thrones for him to sit,

Poems to read, and beds
In which it may please him to rest.

This is the land
The pioneers looked for, shading their eyes
Against the sun—a murmur of serious life.

W. D. Snodgrass

THESE TREES STAND . . .

These trees stand very tall under the heavens.
While *they* stand, if I walk, all stars traverse
This steep celestial gulf their branches chart.
Though lovers stand at sixes and at sevens
While civilizations come down with the curse,
Snodgrass is walking through the universe.

I can't make any world go around *your* house.
But note this moon. Recall how the night nurse
Goes ward-rounds, by the mild, reflective art
Of focusing her flashlight on her blouse.
Your name's safe conduct into love or verse;
Snodgrass is walking through the universe.

Your name's absurd, miraculous as sperm
And as decisive. If you can't coerce
One thing outside yourself, why you're the poet!
What irrefrangible atoms whirl, affirm
Their destiny and form Lucinda's skirts!
She can't make up your mind. Soon as you know it,
Your firmament grows touchable and firm.
If all this world runs battlefield or worse,
Come, let us wipe our glasses on our shirts:
Snodgrass is walking through the universe.

from *HEART'S NEEDLE*

9

I get numb and go in
though the dry ground will not hold

the few dry swirls of snow
and it must not be very cold.
A friend asks how you've been
        and I don't know

or see much right to ask.
Or what use it could be to know.
    In three months since you came
the leaves have fallen and the snow;
your pictures pinned above my desk
        seem much the same.

Somehow I come to find
myself upstairs in the third floor
    museum's halls,
walking to kill my time once more
among the enduring and resigned
        stuffed animals,

where, through a century's
caprice, displacement and
    known treachery between
its wars, they hear some old command
and in their peaceable kingdoms freeze
        to this still scene,

Nature Morte. Here
by the door, its guardian,
    the patchwork dodo stands
where you and your stepsister ran
laughing and pointing. Here, last year,
        you pulled my hands

and had your first, worst quarrel,
so toys were put up on your shelves.
    Here in the first glass cage
the little bobcats arch themselves,
still practicing their snarl
        of constant rage.

The bison, here, immense,
shoves at his calf, brow to brow,
    and looks it in the eye
to see what is it thinking now.
I forced you to obedience;
    I don't know why.

Still the lean lioness
beyond them, on her jutting ledge
    of shale and desert shrub,
stands watching always at the edge,
stands hard and tanned and envious
    above her cub;

with horns locked in tall heather,
two great Olympian Elk stand bound,
    fixed in their lasting hate
till hunger brings them both to ground.
Whom equal weakness binds together
    none shall separate.

Yet separate in the ocean
of broken ice, the white bear reels
    beyond the leathery groups
of scattered, drab Arctic seals
arrested here in violent motion
    like Napoleon's troops.

Our states have stood so long
At war, shaken with hate and dread,
    they are paralyzed at bay;
once we were out of reach, we said,
we would grow reasonable and strong.
    Some other day.

Like the cold men of Rome,
we have won costly fields to sow
    in salt, our only seed.

Nothing but injury will grow.
I write you only the bitter poems
    that you can't read.

    Onan who would not breed
a child to take his brother's bread
    and be his brother's birth,
rose up and left his lawful bed,
went out and spilled his seed
    in the cold earth.

    I stand by the unborn,
by putty-colored children curled
    in jars of alcohol,
that waken to no other world,
unchanging where no eye shall mourn.
    I see the caul

    that wrapped a kitten, dead.
I see the branching, double throat
    of a two-headed foal;
I see the hydrocephalic goat;
here is the curled and swollen head,
    there, the burst skull;

    skin of a limbless calf;
a horse's foetus, mummified;
    mounted and joined forever,
the Siamese twin dogs that ride
belly to belly, half and half,
    that none shall sever.

    I walk among the growths,
by gangrenous tissue, goitre, cysts,
    by fistulas and cancers,
where the malignancy man loathes
is held suspended and persists.
    And I don't know the answers.

The window's turning white.
The world moves like a diseased heart
   packed with ice and snow.
Three months now we have been apart
less than a mile. I cannot fight
   or let you go.

MEMENTOS, i

Sorting out letters and piles of my old
   Cancelled checks, old clippings, and yellow note cards
That meant something once, I happened to find
   Your picture. *That* picture. I stopped there cold
Like a man raking piles of dead leaves in his yard
   Who has turned up a severed hand.

Yet, that first second, I was glad: you stand
   Just as you stood—shy, delicate, slender,
In the long gown of green lace netting and daisies
   That you wore to our first dance. The sight of you stunned
Us all. Our needs seemed simpler, then;
   And our ideals came easy.

Then through the war and those two long years
   Overseas, the Japanese dead in their shacks
Among dishes, dolls, and lost shoes—I carried
   This glimpse of you, there, to choke down my fear,
Prove it had been, that it might come back.
   That was before we got married.

—Before we drained out one another's force
   With lies, self-denial, unspoken regret
And the sick eyes that blame; before the divorce
   And the treachery. Say it: before we met.
Still, I put back your picture. Someday, in due course,
   I will find that it's still there.

THE EXAMINATION

Under the thick beams of that swirly smoking light,
   The black robes are clustering, huddled in together.
Hunching their shoulders, they spread short, broad sleeves like
     night-
   Black grackles' wings and reach out bone-yellow leather-

Y fingers, each to each. And are prepared. Each turns
   His single eye—or since one can't discern their eyes,
That reflective, single, moon-pale disc which burns
   Over each brow—to watch this uncouth shape that lies

Strapped to their table. One probes with his ragged nails
   The slate-sharp calf, explores the thigh and the lean thews
Of the groin. Others raise, red as piratic sails,
   His wing, stretching, trying the pectoral sinews.

One runs his finger down the whet of that cruel
   Golden beak, lifts back the horny lids from the eyes,
Peers down in one bright eye, malign as a jewel
   And steps back suddenly. "He is anaesthetized?"

"He is. He is. Yes. Yes." The tallest of them, bent
   Down by the head, rises. "This drug possesses powers
Sufficient to still all gods in this firmament.
   This is Garuda who was fierce. He's yours for hours.

"We shall continue, please." Now, once again, he bends
   To the skull, and its clamped tissues. Into the cra-
Nial cavity, he plunges both of his hands
   Like obstetric forceps and lifts out the great brain.

Holds it aloft, then gives it to the next who stands
   Beside him. Each, in turn, accepts it, although loath,
Turns it this way, that way, feels it between his hands
   Like a wasp's nest or some sickening outsized growth.

They must decide what thoughts each part of it must think;
    They tap it, then listen beside, each suspect lobe,
Next, with a crow's quill dipped into India ink,
    Mark on its surface, as if on a map or globe,

Those dangerous areas which need to be excised.
    They rinse it, then apply antiseptics to it;
Now, silver saws appear which, inch by inch, slice
    Through its ancient folds and ridges, like thick suet.

It's rinsed, dried, and daubed with thick salves. The smoky saws
    Are scrubbed, resterilized, and polished till they gleam.
The brain is repacked in its case. Pinched in their claws,
    Glimmering needles stitch it up, that leave no seam.

Meantime, one of them has set blinders to the eyes,
    Inserted light packing beneath each of the ears
And caulked the nostrils in. One, with thin twine, ties
    The genitals off. With long wooden-handled shears,

Another chops pinions out of the scarlet wings.
    It's hoped that with disuse he will forget the sky
Or, at least, in time, learn, among other things,
    To fly no higher than his superiors fly.

Well; that's a beginning. The next time, they can split
    His tongue and teach him to talk correctly, can give
Him memory of fine books and choose clothing fit
    For the integrated area where he'll live.

Their candidate may live to give them thanks one day.
    He will recover and may hope for such success
He might return to join their ranks. Bowing away,
    They nod, whispering, "One of ours; one of ours. Yes. Yes."

A FLAT ONE

Old Fritz, on this rotating bed
For seven wasted months you lay

Unfit to move, shrunken, gray,
No good to yourself or anyone
But to be babied—changed and bathed and fed.
At long last, that's all done.

Before each meal, twice every night,
We set pads on your bedsores, shut
Your catheter tube off, then brought
The second canvas-and-black-iron
Bedframe and clamped you in between them, tight,
Scared, so we could turn

You over. We washed you, covered you,
Cut up each bite of meat you ate;
We watched your lean jaws masticate
As ravenously your useless food
As thieves at hard labor in their chains chew
Or insects in the wood.

Such pious sacrifice to give
You all you could demand of pain:
Receive this haddock's body, slain
For you, old tyrant; take this blood
Of a tomato, shed that you might live.
You had that costly food.

You seem to be all finished, so
We'll plug your old recalcitrant anus
And tie up your discouraged penis
In a great, snow-white bow of gauze.
We wrap you, pin you, and cart you down below,
Below, below, because

Your credit has finally run out.
On our steel table, trussed and carved,
You'll find this world's hardworking, starved
Teeth working in your precious skin.
The earth turns, in the end, by turn about
And opens to take you in.

Seven months gone down the drain; thank God
That's through. Throw out the four-by-fours,
Swabsticks, the thick salve for bedsores,
Throw out the diaper pads and drug
Containers, pile the bedclothes in a wad,
     And rinse the cider jug

Half filled with the last urine. Then
Empty out the cotton cans,
Autoclave the bowls and spit pans,
Unhook the pumps and all the red
Tubes—catheter, suction, oxygen;
     Next, wash the empty bed.

—All this Dark Age machinery
On which we had tormented you
To life. Last, we collect the few
Belongings: snapshots, some odd bills,
Your mail, and half a pack of Luckies we
     Won't light you after meals.

Old man, these seven months you've lain
Determined—not that you would live—
Just to not die. No one would give
You one chance you could ever wake
From that first night, much less go well again,
     Much less go home and make

Your living; how could you hope to find
A place for yourself in all creation?—
Pain was your only occupation.
     And pain that should content and will
A man to give it up, nerved you to grind
     Your clenched teeth, breathing, till

Your skin broke down, your calves went flat
Your legs lost all sensation. Still,
You took enough morphine to kill

A strong man. Finally, nitrogen
Mustard: you could last two months after that;
    It would kill you then.

Even then you wouldn't quit.
Old soldier, yet you must have known
Inside the animal had grown
Sick of the world, made up its mind
To stop. Your mind ground on its separate
    Way, merciless and blind,

Into these last weeks when the breath
Would only come in fits and starts
That puffed out your sections like the parts
Of some enormous, damaged bug.
You waited, not for life, not for your death,
    Just for the deadening drug

That made your life seem bearable.
You still whispered you would not die.
Yet in the nights I heard you cry
Like a whipped child; in fierce old age
You whimpered, tears stood on your gun-metal
    Blue cheeks shaking with rage

And terror. So much pain would fill
Your room that when I left I'd pray
That if I came back the next day
I'd find you gone. You stayed for me—
Nailed to your own rapacious, stiff self-will.
    You've shook loose, finally.

They'd say this was a worthwhile job
Unless they tried it. It is mad
To throw our good lives after bad;
    Waste time, drugs, and our minds, while strong
Men starve. How many young men did we rob
    To keep you hanging on?

I can't think we did you much good.
Well, when you died, none of us wept.
You killed for us, and so we kept
You, because we need to earn our pay.
No. We'd still have to help you try. We would
          Have killed for you today.

A FRIEND

I walk into your house, a friend.
Your kids swarm up my steep hillsides
Or swing in my branches. Your boy rides
Me for his horsie; we pretend
Some troll threatens our lady fair.
I swing him squealing through the air
And down. Just what could I defend?

I tuck them in, sometimes, at night.
That's one secret we never tell.
Giggling in their dark room, they yell
They love me. Their father, home tonight,
Sees your girl curled up on my knee
And tells her "git"—she's bothering me.
I nod; she'd better think he's right.

Once they're in bed, he calls you "dear."
The boob-tube shows some hokum on
Adultery and loss; we yawn
Over a stale joke book and beer
Till it's your bedtime. I must leave.
I watch that squat toad pluck your sleeve.
As always, you stand shining near

Your window. I stand, Prince of Lies
Who's seen bliss; now I can drive back
Home past wreck and carlot, past shack

Slum and steelmill reddening the skies,
Past drive-ins, the hot pits where our teens
Fingerfuck and that huge screen's
Images fill their vacant eyes.

Gary Snyder

MILTON BY FIRELIGHT

Piute Creek, August 1955

"O hell, what do mine eyes
        with grief behold?"
Working with an old
Singlejack miner, who can sense
The vein and cleavage
In the very guts of rock, can
Blast granite, build
Switchbacks that last for years
Under the beat of snow, thaw, mule-hooves.
What use, Milton, a silly story
Of our lost general parents,
        eaters of fruit?

The Indian, the chainsaw boy,
And a string of six mules
Came riding down to camp
Hungry for tomatoes and green apples.
Sleeping in saddle-blankets
Under a bright night-sky
Han River slantwise by morning.
Jays squall
Coffee boils

In ten thousand years the Sierras
Will be dry and dead, home of the scorpion.
Ice-scratched slabs and bent trees.
No paradise, no fall,
Only the weathering land
The wheeling sky,

Man, with his Satan
Scouring the chaos of the mind.
Oh Hell!

Fire down
Too dark to read, miles from a road
The bell-mare clangs in the meadow
That packed dirt for a fill-in
Scrambling through loose rocks
On an old trail
All of a summer's day.

A STONE GARDEN

1

Japan a great stone garden in the sea.
Echoes of hoes and weeding,
Centuries of leading hill-creeks down
To ditch and pool in fragile knee-deep fields.
Stone-cutter's chisel and a whanging saw,
Leafy sunshine rustling on a man
Chipping a foot-square rough hinoki beam;
I thought I heard an axe chop in the woods
It broke the dream; and woke up dreaming on a train.
It must have been a thousand years ago
In some old mountain sawmill of Japan.
A horde of excess poets and unwed girls
And I that night prowled Tokyo like a bear
Tracking the human future
Of intelligence and despair.

2

I recollect a girl I thought I knew.
Little black-haired bobcut children
Scatter water on the dusty morning street—
& walked a hundred nights in summer

Seeing in open doors and screens
The thousand postures of all human fond
Touches and gestures, glidings, nude,
The oldest and nakedest women more the sweet,
And saw there first old withered breasts
Without an inward wail of sorrow and dismay
Because impermanence and destructiveness of time
In truth means only, lovely women age—
But with the noble glance of I Am Loved
From children and from crones, time is destroyed.
The cities rise and fall and rise again
From storm and quake and fire and bomb,
The glittering smelly ricefields bloom,
And all that growing up and burning down
Hangs in the void a little knot of sound.

3

Thinking about a poem I'll never write.
With gut on wood and hide, and plucking thumb,
Grope and stutter for the words, invent a tune,
In any tongue, this moment one time true
Be wine or blood or rhythm drives it through—
A leap of words to things and there it stops.
Creating empty caves and tools in shops
And holy domes, and nothing you can name;
The long old chorus blowing underfoot
Makes high wild notes of mountains in the sea.
O Muse, a goddess gone astray
Who warms the cow and makes the wise man sane,
(& even madness gobbles demons down)
Then dance through jewelled trees & lotus crowns
For Narahito's lover, the crying plover,
For babies grown and childhood homes
And moving, moving, on through scenes and towns
Weep for the crowds of men
Like birds gone south forever.
The long-lost hawk of Yakamochi and Thoreau

Flits over yonder hill, the hand is bare,
The noise of living families fills the air.

4

What became of the child we never had—
Delight binds man to birth, to death,
—Let's gather in the home—for soon we part—
(The daughter is in school, the son's at work)
& silver fish-scales coat the hand, the board;
The charcoal glowing underneath the eaves,
Squatting and fanning til the rice is steamed,
All our friends and children come to eat.
This marriage never dies. Delight
Crushes it down and builds it all again
With flesh and wood and stone,
The woman there—she is not old or young.

Allowing such distinctions to the mind:
A formal garden made by fire and time.

Red Sea December 1957

from *MYTHS AND TEXTS, III*

14

A skin-bound bundle of clutchings
          unborn and with no place to go
Balanced on the boundless compassion
Of diatoms, lava, and chipmunks.

Love, let it be,
Is a sacrifice
               knees, the cornered eyes
Tea on a primus stove after a cold swim

Intricate doors and clocks, the clothes
    we stand in—
Gaps between seedings, the right year,
Green shoots in the marshes
Creeks in the proper directions
Hills in proportion,
Astrologers, go-betweens present,
        a marriage has been.

Walked all day through live oak and manzanita,
Scrabbling through dust down Tamalpais—
Thought of high mountains;
Looked out on a sea of fog.
Two of us, carrying packs.

15

Stone-flake and salmon.
The pure, sweet, straight-splitting
        with a ping
Red cedar of the thick coast valleys
Shake-blanks on the mashed ferns
        the charred logs
Fireweed and bees
An old burn, by new alder
Creek on smooth stones,
Back there a Tarheel logger farm.
(High country fir still hunched in snow)
From Siwash strawberry-pickers in the Skagit
Down to the boys at Sac,
Living by the river
      riding flatcars to Fresno,
Across the whole country
Steep towns, flat towns, even New York,
And oceans and Europe & libraries & galleries
And the factories they make rubbers in
This whole spinning show
      (among others)
Watched by the Mt. Sumeru L.O.

From the middle of the universe
& them with no radio.
"What is imperfect is best"
   silver scum on the trout's belly
   rubs off on your hand.
It's all falling or burning—
   rattle of boulders
   steady dribbling of rocks down cliffs
   bark chips in creeks
Porcupine chawed here—
       Smoke
From Tillamook a thousand miles
Soot and hot ashes. Forest fires.
Upper Skagit burned I think 1919
Smoke covered all northern Washington.
   lightning strikes, flares,
Blossoms a fire on the hill.
Smoke like clouds. Blotting the sun
Stinging the eyes.
The hot seeds steam underground
   still alive.

      16

"Wash me on home, mama"
     —song of the Kelp.
A chief's wife
Sat with her back to the sun
On the sandy beach, shredding cedar-bark.
Her fingers were slender
She didn't eat much.

"Get foggy
We're going out to dig
Buttercup roots"

Dream, Dream,

Earth! those beings living on your surface

none of them disappearing, will all be transformed.
When I have spoken to them
when they have spoken to me, from that moment on,
their words and their bodies which they
usually use to move about with, will all change.
I will not have heard them. Signed,

(   )

Coyote

17

the text

Sourdough mountain called a fire in:
Up Thunder Creek, high on a ridge.
Hiked eighteen hours, finally found
A snag and a hundred feet around on fire:
All afternoon and into night
Digging the fire line
Falling the burning snag
It fanned sparks down like shooting stars
Over the dry woods, starting spot-fires
Flaring in wind up Skagit valley
From the Sound.
Toward morning it rained.
We slept in mud and ashes,
Woke at dawn, the fire was out,
The sky was clear, we saw
The last glimmer of the morning star.

FOUR POEMS FOR ROBIN

Siwashing it out once in Siuslaw National Forest

I slept under   rhododendron
All night   blossoms fell
Shivering on   a sheet of cardboard
Feet stuck   in my pack

Hands deep   in my pockets
Barely   able   to   sleep.
I remembered   when we were in school
Sleeping together   in a big warm bed
We were   the youngest lovers
When we broke up   we were still nineteen.
Now our   friends are married
You teach   school back east
I dont mind   living this way
Green hills   the long blue beach
But sometimes   sleeping in the open
I think back   when I had you.

A spring night in Shokoku-ji

Eight years ago this May
We walked under cherry blossoms
At night in an orchard in Oregon.
All that I wanted then
Is forgotten now, but you.
Here in the night
In a garden of the old capitol
I feel the trembling ghost of Yugao
I remember your cool body
Naked under a summer cotton dress.

An autumn morning in Shokoku-ji

Last night watching the Pleiades,
Breath smoking in the moonlight,
Bitter memory like vomit
Choked my throat.
I unrolled a sleeping bag
On mats on the porch
Under thick autumn stars.
In dream you appeared
(Three times in nine years)
Wild, cold, and accusing.

I woke shamed and angry:
The pointless wars of the heart.
Almost dawn. Venus and Jupiter.
The first time I have
Ever seen them close.

December at Yase

You said, that October,
In the tall dry grass by the orchard
When you chose to be free,
"Again someday, maybe ten years."

After college I saw you
One time. You were strange.
And I was obsessed with a plan.

Now ten years and more have
Gone by: I've always known
            where you were—
I might have gone to you
Hoping to win your love back.
You still are single.

I didn't.
I thought I must make it alone. I
Have done that.

Only in dream, like this dawn,
Does the grave, awed intensity
Of our young love
Return to my mind, to my flesh.

We had what the others
All crave and seek for;
We left it behind at nineteen.

I feel ancient, as though I had
Lived many lives.

And may never now know
If I am a fool
Or have done what my
     karma demands.

Mark Strand

THE TUNNEL

A man has been standing
in front of my house
for days. I peek at him
from the living room
window and at night,
unable to sleep,
I shine my flashlight
down on the lawn.
He is always there.

After a while
I open the front door
just a crack and order
him out of my yard.
He narrows his eyes
and moans. I slam
the door and dash back
to the kitchen, then up
to the bedroom, then down.

I weep like a schoolgirl
and make obscene gestures
through the window. I
write large suicide notes
and place them so he
can read them easily.
I destroy the living
room furniture to prove
I own nothing of value.

When he seems unmoved

I decide to dig a tunnel
to a neighboring yard.
I seal the basement off
from the upstairs with
a brick wall. I dig hard
and in no time the tunnel
is done. Leaving my pick
and shovel below,

I come out in front of a house
and stand there too tired to
move or even speak, hoping
someone will help me.
I feel I'm being watched
and sometimes I hear
a man's voice,
but nothing is done
and I have been waiting for days.

EATING POETRY

Ink runs from the corners of my mouth.
There is no happiness like mine.
I have been eating poetry.

The librarian does not believe what she sees.
Her eyes are sad
and she walks with her hands in her dress.

The poems are gone.
The light is dim.
The dogs are on the basement stairs and coming up.

Their eyeballs roll,
their blond legs burn like brush.
The poor librarian begins to stamp her feet and weep.

She does not understand.
When I get on my knees and lick her hand,
she screams.

I am a new man.
I snarl at her and bark.
I romp with joy in the bookish dark.

May Swenson

WORKING ON WALL STREET

What's left of the sunset's watered blood
settles between the slabs of Wall Street.
Winter rubs the sky bruise-blue as flesh.
We head down into the subway, glad
the cars are padded with bodies so we
keep warm. Emptied from tall closets
where we work, on the days' shelves
reached by elevators, the heap of us,
pressed by iron sides, dives forward under
the city—parcels shipped out in a trunk.

The train climbs from its cut to the trestle.
Sunset's gone. Those slabs across the murky
river have shrunk to figurines, reflecting
the blush of neon—a dainty tableau, all
pink, on the dresser-top of Manhattan—
eclipsed as we sink into the tunnel.
The train drops and flattens for the long
bore under Brooklyn.

Night, a hiatus hardly real, tomorrow
this double rut of steel will racket us back
to the city. We, packages in the trade
made day after day, will tumble out of
hatches on The Street, to be met by swags
of wind that scupper off those roofs
(their upper windows blood-filled by the sun.)
Delivered into lobbies, clapped into upgoing
cages, sorted to our compartments, we'll be
stamped once more for our wages.

SATANIC FORM

Numerals forkmarks of Satan
Triangles circles squares
hieroglyphs of death
Things invented
abortions smelling of the forge
licked to gruesome smoothness by the lathe
Things metallic or glass
frozen twisted flattened
stretched to agonized bubbles
Bricks beams receptacles vehicles
forced through fire hatched to unwilling form
O blasphemies
Time caught in a metal box
Incongruous the rigid clucking tongue
the needled hands the 12-eyed face
against the open window past which drops the night
like a dark lake on end or flowing hair
Night unanimous over all the city
The knuckled fist of the heart opening and closing
Flower and song not cursed with symmetry
Cloud and shadow not doomed to shape and fixity
The intricate body of man without rivet or nail
on the terrible skirl of the screw
O these are blessed
Satanic form geometry of death
The lariat around the neck of space
The particles of chaos in the clock
The bottle of the yellow liquor light
that circumvents the sifting down of night
O love the juice in the green stem growing
we cannot synthesize
It corrodes in phials and beakers
evaporates in the hot breath of industry
escapes to the air and the dew
returns to the root of the unborn flower
O Satan cheated of your power

ALMANAC

The hammer struck my nail, instead of nail.
A moon flinched into being. Omen-black,
it began its trail. Risen from horizon
on my thumb (no longer numb and indigo)
it waxed yellow, waned to a sliver that now
sets white, here at the rim I cut tonight.

I make it disappear, but mark its voyage
over my little oval ceiling that again
is cloudless, pink and clear. In the dark
quarter-inch of this moon before it arrived
at my nail's tip, an unmanned airship
dived 200 miles to the hem of space, and
vanished. At the place of Pharaoh Cheops'
tomb (my full moon floating yellow)
a boat for ferrying souls to the sun
was disclosed in a room sealed 5000 years.

Reaching whiteness, this moon-speck waned
while an April rained. Across the street,
a vine crept over brick up 14 feet. And
Einstein (who said there is no hitching
post in the universe) at 77 turned ghost.

NIGHT PRACTICE

I
will
remember
with my breath
to make a mountain,
with my sucked-in breath
a valley, with my pushed-out
breath a mountain. I will make
a valley wider than the whisper, I
will make a higher mountain than the cry;
will with my will breathe a mountain, I will
with my will breathe a valley. I will push out a
mountain, suck in a valley, deeper than the shout
YOU MUST DIE, harder, heavier, sharper, a mountain
than the truth YOU MUST DIE. I will remember. My breath
will make a mountain. My will will remember to will. I, suck-
ing, pushing, I will breathe a valley, I will breathe a mountain.

CARDINAL IDEOGRAMS

0   A mouth.   Can blow or breathe,
    be funnel, or Hello.

1   A glass blade or a cut.

2   A question seated.   And a proud
    bird's neck.

3   Shallow mitten for two-fingered hand.

4   Three-cornered hut
    on one stilt.   Sometimes built
    so the roof gapes.

5   A policeman.   Polite.
    Wearing visored cap.

6   O unrolling,
    tape of ambiguous length
    on which is written the mystery
    of everything curly.

7   A step,
    detached from its stair.

8   The universe in diagram:
    A cosmic hourglass.
    (Note enigmatic shape,
    absence of any valve of origin,
    how end overlaps beginning.)
    Unknotted like a shoelace
    and whipped back and forth,
    can serve as a model of time.

9   Lorgnette for the right eye.
    In England or if you are Alice
    the stem is on the left.

10 A glass blade or a cut
    companioned by a mouth.
    Open?   Open.   Shut?   Shut.

THE SECRET IN THE CAT

I took my cat apart
to see what made him purr.
Like an electric clock
or like the snore

of a warming kettle,
something fizzed and sizzled in him.

Was he a soft car,
the engine bubbling sound?

Was there a wire beneath his fur,
or humming throttle?
I undid his throat.
Within was no stir.

I opened up his chest
as though it were a door:
no whisk or rattle there.
I lifted off his skull:

no hiss or murmur.
I halved his little belly
but found no gear,
no cause for static.

So I replaced his lid,
laced his little gut.
His heart into his vest I slid
and buttoned up his throat.

His tail rose to a rod
and beckoned to the air.
Some voltage made him vibrate
warmer than before.

Whiskers and a tail:
perhaps they caught
some radar code
emitted as a pip, a dot-and-dash

of woolen sound.
My cat a kind of tuning fork?—
amplifier?—telegraph?—
doing secret signal work?

His eyes elliptic tubes:
there's a message in his stare.
I stroke him
but cannot find the dial.

Charles Tomlinson

THROUGH BINOCULARS

In their congealed light
We discover that what we had taken for a face
Has neither eyes nor mouth,
But only the impersonality of anatomy.

Silencing movement,
They withdraw life.

Definition grows clear-cut, but bodiless,
Withering by a dimension.

To see thus
Is to ignore the revenge of light on shadow,
To confound both in a brittle and false union.

This fictive extension into madness
Has a kind of bracing effect:
That normality is, after all, desirable
One can no longer doubt having experienced its opposite.

Binoculars are the last phase in a romanticism:
The starkly mad vision, not mortal,
But dangling one in a vicarious, momentary idiocy.

To dispense with them
Is to make audible the steady roar of evening,
Withdrawing in slow ripples of orange,
Like the retreat of water from sea-caves.

TRAMONTANA AT LERICI

Today, should you let fall a glass, it would
   Disintegrate, played off with such keenness
Against the cold's resonance (the sounds
   Hard, separate and distinct, dropping away
In a diminishing cadence) that you might swear
   This was the imitation of glass falling.

Leaf-dapples sharpen. Emboldened by this clarity
   The minds of artificers would turn prismatic
Running on lace perforated in crisp wafers
   That could cut like steel. Constitutions,
Drafted under this fecund chill would be annulled
   For the strictness of their equity, the moderation of their pity.

At evening, one is alarmed by such definition
   In as many lost greens as one will give glances to recover,
As many again which the landscape
   Absorbing into the steady dusk, condenses
From aquamarine to that slow indigo-pitch
   Where the light and twilight abondon themselves.

And the chill grows. In this air
   Unfit for politicians and romantics
Dark hardens from blue, effacing the windows:
   A tangible block, it will be no accessory
To that which does not concern it. One is ignored
   By so much cold suspended in so much night.

THE MEDITERRANEAN

I

In this country of grapes
Where the architecture
Plays musical interludes, flays
The emotions with the barest statement
Or, confusing the issue and the beholder,
Bewilders with an excessive formality,
There is also the sea.

II

           The sea
Whether it is "wrinkled" and "crawls"
Or pounds, plunders, rounding
On itself in thunderous showers, a
Broken, bellowing foam canopy
Rock-riven and driven wild
By its own formless griefs—the sea
Carries, midway, its burning stripe of light.

III

This country of grapes
Is a country, also, of trains, planes and gasworks.
"Tramway and palace" rankles. It is an idea
Neither the guidebook nor the imagination
Tolerates. The guidebook half lies
Of "twenty minutes in a comfortable bus"
Of "rows of cypresses, an
Uninterrupted series of matchless sights."
The imagination cannot lie. It bites brick;
Says: "This is steel—I will taste steel.
Bred on a lie, I am merely
Guidebooks, advertisements, politics."

The sea laps by the railroad tracks.
To have admitted this also defines the sea.

REFLECTIONS

Like liquid shadows. The ice is thin
   Whose mirror smears them as it intercepts
Withdrawing colors; and where the crust,
   As if a skin livid with tautening scars,
Whitens, cracks, it steals from these deformations
   A style too tenuous for the image. A mirror lies, and
Flawed like this, may even lie with art,
   With reticence: "I exaggerate nothing,
For the reflections—scarcely half you see—
   Tell nothing of what you feel." Nature is blind
Like habit. Distrust them. We, since no mirrors,
   Are free both to question this deployment
And to arrange it—what we reflect
   Being what we choose. Though without deference,
We are grateful. When we perceive, as keen
   As the bridge itself, a bridge inlaying the darkness
Of smooth water, our delight acknowledges our debt—
   To nature, from whom we choose;
And, fencing that fullness back, to habit,
   The unsheathed image piercing our winter sleep.

PARING THE APPLE

There are portraits and still-lives.

And there is paring the apple.

And then? Paring it slowly,
From under cool-yellow
Cold-white emerging. And . . . ?

The spring of concentric peel

Unwinding off white,
The blade hidden, dividing.

There are portraits and still-lives
And the first, because 'human'
Does not excel the second, and
Neither is less weighted
With a human gesture, than paring the apple
With a human stillness.

The cool blade
Severs between coolness, apple-rind
Compelling a recognition.

AT BARSTOW

Nervy with neons, the main drag
was all there was. A placeless place.
A faint flavour of Mexico in the tacos
tasting of gasoline. Truck refuelled
before taking off through space. Someone lived
in the houses with their houseyards wired
like tiny Belsens. The Götterdämmerung
would be like this. No funeral pyres, no choirs
of lost trombones. An Untergang
without a clang, without
a glimmer of gone glory
however dimmed. At the motel desk
was a photograph of Roy Rogers
signed. It was here
he made a stay. He did not
ride away on Trigger
through the high night, the tilted
Pleiades overhead, the polestar low, no
going off until
the eyes of beer-cans
had ceased to glint at him

and the desert darknesses
had quenched the neons. He was spent.
He was content. Down he lay.
The passing trucks patrolled his sleep,
the shifted gears contrived
a muffled fugue against the fading of his day
and his dustless, undishonoured stetson rode
beside the bed,
glowed in the pulsating, never-final twilight
there, at that execrable conjunction
of gasoline and desert air.

THE CAVERN

Obliterate
mythology as you unwind
this mountain-interior
into the negative-dark mind,
as there
the gypsum's snow
the limestone stair
and boneyard landscape grow
into the identity of flesh.

Pulse of the water-drop,
veils and scales, fins
and flakes of the forming
leprous rock,
how should these
inhuman, turn
human with such chill affinities.

Hard to the hand,
these mosses not of moss,
but nostrils, pits
of eyes, faces
in flight and prints

of feet where no feet ever were,
elude the mind's
hollow that would contain
this canyon within a mountain.

Not far
enough from the familiar,
press
in under a deeper dark until
the curtained sex
the arch the streaming buttress
have become
the self's unnameable and shaping home.

Chris Wallace-Crabbe

IN LIGHT AND DARKNESS

To the noonday eye, light seems an ethical agent,
Straight from the shoulder, predictable, terribly quick, though
It climbs in a curve to space's unlikely limit,
    Thus posing a problem for mathematicians and God,
Whatever He turns out to be and wherever His dwelling.
Rich is the clotting of gold in the late afternoon or
Turning to twilight, one last blaze of watery colour
    Where man can project his false dreams in figures of light,
Pretending that all his environment loyally loves him,
Seas of ice and buring plains.
                        Too easy
Bending nature before us, but light is defiant
    Coming by night from dead stars with terrible speed.
So is our planet rebuked, and we meet in mirrors
Desperate masks, eyes of imprisoned strangers
And lips that open to say, "We are only mirages,"
    While the lawns outside are green and the roses real.

You dub the sun a realist? Then it will plague you,
Wading with stork-legs into the green water,
Lending the oak-bole moss its leopard shadows
    Or streaking paddocks darkly with sunset sheep
Fifty feet long.
                  Nothing is quite so rococo
As dawnlight caught on a fishscale formation of cirrus,
Nor quite so romantic as one gilded westering biplane.
    We just don't live in a hard intellectual glare.
No one, of course, endures darkness or daylight entirely:
Cyclic change betrays our terrestrial journey
And what looked like trees at dawn turn out to be crosses,
    Suddenly black as the florid sun goes down,

And maybe at midnight resemble gallows or statues
As we slip past, childlike, alone.

                No wonder
Sly poets admiringly use, but will not warm to
    The subtle machines that teach our world to spin.
These are too steady for reverence: gods must be changeable
Since worship is saved for what we cannot govern;
Gods push up grass, channel the dense sap through pine-boughs
    And amass the pewter cloudbanks of summer storm.

Once I awoke, a child in a chill mountain morning,
To see the small town—undreamed transfiguration—
Mantled in white, its slate and stone and timber
    Bright with that foreign cloak of innocence.
And I walked into old-world beauty; the gilt sun rising
Fell in a garden where time itself was congealing
As we shaped wonderful igloos under the stringybarks
    And took no account of thaw. But noon came on.
Something was lost in the brown receding slush there
Which has not returned, something other than childhood:
A notion, rather, of clear crystalline standards
    Freezing life to one shape, like a photograph.

Yet this is the point:
                a photograph leaves out living
For Eton crops, old blazers, baptismal lace or
Some late-Victorian smile turned stiff and waxy,
    All arabesques, but never the heart of the thing;
Which is neither good nor bad, but one maze of motion
Through which we dance, into and out of the darkness
To tireless music: motes in the curled winds' breathing
    And more than motes, faced with the corners of choice.
And so at night below all the brilliant clusters
Of lamps in the sky, the living, dead and dying
Poised in their dance, I cling to the crust here stolidly
    And pray for a perfect day.

                    Out in the cold
Of hoarfrost and starlight, we fear for tomorrow's choosing

And cherish dreams made in meticulous patterns;
But come tomorrow, we will neither be Christ nor Gandhi
     But will breathe this common air and rejoice with the birds.

All that I ask is that myriad lights, ever changing,
Continue to play on this great rind of ranges and valleys,
Flooding the vision of dreaming dwellers in cities
     Who walk out in summer pursuing something to praise:
     We will neither be simple nor clear till the end of our days.

A WINTRY MANIFESTO

It was the death of Satan first of all,
The knowledge that earth holds though kingdoms fall,
     Inured us to a stoic resignation,
     To making the most of a shrunken neighbourhood;

And what we drew on was not gold or fire,
No cross, not cloven hoof about the pyre,
     But painful, plain, contracted observations:
     The gesture of a hand, dip of a bough

Or seven stubborn words drawn close together
As a hewn charm against the shifting weather.
     Our singing was intolerably sober
     Mistrusting every trill of artifice.

Whatever danced on needle-points, we knew
That we had forged the world we stumbled through
     And, if a stripped wind howled through sighing alleys,
     Built our own refuge in a flush of pride

Knowing that all our gifts were for construction—
Timber to timber groined in every section—
     And knowing, too, purged of the sense of evil,
     These were the walls our folly would destroy.

We dreamed, woke, doubted, wept for fading stars
And then projected brave new avatars,
    Triumphs of reason. Yet a whole dimension
    Had vanished from the chambers of the mind,

And paramount among the victims fled,
Shrunken and pale, the grim king of the dead;
    Withdrawn to caverns safely beyond our sounding
    He waits as a Pretender for his call,

Which those who crave him can no longer give.
Men are the arbiters of how they live,
    And, stooped by millstones of authority,
    They welcome tyrants in with open arms.

Now in the shadows of unfriendly trees
We number leaves, discern faint similes
    And learn to praise whatever is imperfect
    As the true breeding-ground for honesty,

Finding our heroism in rejection
Of bland Utopias and of thieves' affection:
    Our greatest joy to mark an outline truly
    And know the piece of earth on which we stand.

WIND AND CHANGE

It is the body swaying on its stalk,
The living bloom aware of light,
Even those hands in motion as in leaf,
That shake me so
Who draw near in disembodiment, delight
Even: crossing the furry lawn,
Butting through wind, impelled by some belief
In the dazzling rays of a world made fresh.
Song, even tree,
Are imperfect analogies

For green assertion in the wind's teeth,
For all this warmth in the day's eye,
For everything disordered, all in leaf,
Laughing and blowing.

James Wright

A PRESENTATION OF TWO BIRDS TO MY SON

Chicken. How shall I tell you what it is,
And why it does not float with tanagers?
Its ecstasy is dead, it does not care.
Its children huddle underneath its wings,
And altogether lounge against the shack,
Warm in the slick tarpaulin, smug and soft.

You must not fumble in your mind
The genuine ecstasy of climbing birds
With that dull fowl.
When your grandfather held it by the feet
And laid the skinny neck across
The ragged chopping block,
The flop of wings, the jerk of the red comb
Were a dumb agony,
Stupid and meaningless. It was no joy
To leave the body beaten underfoot;
Life was a flick of corn, a steady roost.
Chicken. The sound is plain.

Look up and see the swift above the trees.
How shall I tell you why he always veers
And banks around the shaken sleeve of air,
Away from ground? He hardly flies on brains;
Pockets of air impale his hollow bones.
He leans against the rainfall or the sun.

You must not mix this pair of birds
Together in your mind before you know
That both are clods.
What makes the chimney swift approach the sky

Is ecstasy, a kind of fire
That beats the bones apart
And lets the fragile feathers close with air.
Flight too is agony,
Stupid and meaningless. Why should it be joy
To leave the body beaten underfoot,
To mold the limbs against the wind, and join
Those clean dark glides of Dionysian birds?
The flight is deeper than your father, boy.

MORNING HYMN TO A DARK GIRL

Summoned to desolation by the dawn,
I climb the bridge over the water, see
The Negro mount the driver's cabin and wave
Goodbye to the glum cop across the canal,
Goodbye to the flat face and empty eyes
Made human one more time. That uniform
Shivers and dulls against the pier, is stone.

Now in the upper world, the buses drift
Over the bridge, the gulls collect and fly,
Blown by the rush of rose; aseptic girls
Powder their lank deliberate faces, mount
The fog under the billboards. Over the lake
The windows of the rich waken and yawn.
Light blows across the city, dune on dune.

Caught by the scruff of the neck, and thrown out here
To the pale town, to the stone, to burial,
I celebrate you, Betty, flank and breast
Rich to the yellow silk of bed and floors;
Now half awake, your body blossoming trees;
One arm beneath your neck, your legs uprisen,
You blow dark thighs back, back into the dark.

Your shivering ankles skate the scented air;

Betty, burgeoning your golden skin, you poise
Tracing gazelles and tigers on your breasts,
Deep in the jungle of your bed you drowse;
Fine muscles of the rippling panthers move
And snuggle at your calves; under your arms
Mangoes and melons yearn; and glittering slowly,
Quick parakeets trill in your heavy trees,
O everywhere, Betty, between your boughs.

Pity the rising dead who fear the dark.
Soft Betty, locked from snickers in a dark
Brothel, dream on; scatter the yellow corn
Into the wilderness, and sleep all day.
For the leopards leap into the open grass,
Bananas, lemons fling air, fling odor, fall.
And, gracing darkly the dark light, you flow
Out of the grove to laugh at dreamy boys,
You greet the river with a song so low
No lover on a boat can hear, you slide
Silkily to the water, where you rinse
Your fluted body, fearless; though alive
Orangutans sway from the leaves and gaze,
Crocodiles doze along the oozy shore.

THE ASSIGNATION

After the winter thawed away, I rose,
Remembering what you said. Below the field
Where I was dead, the crinkled leaf and blade
Summoned my body, told me I must go.
Across the road I saw some other dead
Revive their little fires, and bow the head
To someone still alive and long ago.
Low in the haze a pall of smoke arose.

Inside the moon's hollow is a hale gray man
Who washed his hands, and waved me where to go:

Up the long hill, the mound of lunar snow,
Around three lapping pebbles, over the crossed
Arms of an owl nailed to the southern sky.
I spun three times about, I scattered high,
Over my shoulder, clouds of salt and dust.
The earth began to clear. I saw a man.

He said the sun was falling toward the trees,
The picnic nearly over. Small on the lake
The sails were luring lightning out of dark,
While quieter people guided slim canoes.
I hid in bushes, shy. Already cars
Shuttled away, the earliest evening stars
Blurred in a cloud. A lone child left his shoes
Half in the sand, and slept beneath the trees.

With fires demolished, everybody gone
To root in bushes, congregate by trees
Or haul the yellow windows down to haze,
I lost my way. Water in water fell,
The badgers nibbled rootlets up the shore,
For dancing more than food, where long before
Women had gossiped. Chanting a soft farewell,
Canaries swung. Then everything was gone.

No hurry for me there, I let my dress
Fall to the lawn, the pleasure of the silk
Wind with the subtle grass, berries and milk
Of skin sweeten me. Snuggling, I lay prone,
Barren yet motherly for what might come
Out of the emptied branches, man or flame.
I shivered slightly. Everything was gone,
Everyone gone. I kicked aside my dress.

O then it was you I waited for, to hold
The soft leaves of my bones between your hands
And warm them back to life, to fashion wands
Out of my shining arms. O it was you
I loved before my dying and long after,

You, you I could not find. The air fell softer,
My snatch of breath gave out, but no one blew
My name in hallowed weeds. Lonely to hold

Some hand upon me, lest it float away
And be as dead as I, thrown in a sack
Of air to drown in air, I rose, lay back
In trees, and died again. The spiders care
For trellises they hold against the sky,
Except for walls of air the houses die
And fall; and only for my flesh of air
Your flesh of earth would lean and drift away;

But you cared nothing, living, false to me.
What could I do but take a daemon then
And slouch about in dust, eager for pain
Or anything, to keep your memory clear?
A thing came down from the dark air on wings
And rummaged at my limbs, to hold my wings
Down in the dirt; I could not see for fear.
The thing withdrew, full of the dark and me.

And I was riven. Even my poor ghost
Can never stand beside your window now;
I stir the wind, I chatter at a bough,
But make no sound. Your cowardice may keep
You from your assignation with my ghost,
The love you promised me when I was dust,
Not air. And yet I cannot even sleep,
I cannot die, but I will feel my ghost

Driven to find this orchard every year,
This picnic ground, and wait till everyone
Tires of the sundown, turns the headlights on,
To float them off like moths into the dark.
I will stand up to strip my hunger off,
And stare, and mumble, knowing all your love
Is cut beside my name on the white rock,
While you forget the promise and the year.

You sat beside the bed, you took my hands;
And when I lay beyond all speech, you said,
You swore to love me after I was dead,
To meet me in a grove and love me still,
Love the white air, the shadow where it lay.
Dear love, I called your name in air today,
I saw the picnic vanish down the hill,
And waved the moon awake, with empty hands.

A BLESSING

Just off the highway to Rochester, Minnesota,
Twilight bounds softly forth on the grass.
And the eyes of those two Indian ponies
Darken with kindness.
They have come gladly out of the willows
To welcome my friend and me.
We step over the barbed wire into the pasture
Where they have been grazing all day, alone.
They ripple tensely, they can hardly contain their
        happiness
That we have come.
They bow shyly as wet swans. They love each other.
There is no loneliness like theirs.
At home once more,
They begin munching the young tufts of spring in the
        darkness.
I would like to hold the slenderer one in my arms,
For she has walked over to me
And nuzzled my left hand.
She is black and white,
Her mane falls wild on her forehead,
And the light breeze moves me to caress her long ear
That is delicate as the skin over a girl's wrist.
Suddenly I realize
That if I stepped out of my body I would break
Into blossom.

TO THE EVENING STAR:
CENTRAL MINNESOTA

Under the water tower at the edge of town
A huge Airedale ponders a long ripple
In the grass fields beyond.
Miles off, a whole grove silently
Flies up into the darkness.
One light comes on in the sky,
One lamp on the prairie.

Beautiful daylight of the body, your hands carry seashells.
West of this wide plain.
Animals wilder than ours
Come down from the green mountains in the darkness.
Now they can see you, they know
The open meadows are safe.

BEGINNING

The moon drops one or two feathers into the field.
The dark wheat listens.
Be still.
Now.
There they are, the moon's young, trying
Their wings.
Between trees, a slender woman lifts up the lovely shadow
Of her face, and now she steps into the air, now she is gone
Wholly, into the air.
I stand alone by an elder tree, I do not dare breathe
Or move.
I listen.
The wheat leans back toward its own darkness,
And I lean toward mine.

THE JEWEL

There is this cave
In the air behind my body
That nobody is going to touch:
A cloister, a silence
Closing around a blossom of fire.
When I stand upright in the wind,
My bones turn to dark emeralds.

TWO HANGOVERS

NUMBER ONE

I slouch in bed.
Beyond the streaked trees of my window,
All groves are bare.
Locusts and poplars changed to unmarried women
Sorting slate from anthracite
Between railroad ties:
The yellow-bearded winter of the depression
Is still alive somewhere, an old man
Counting his collection of bottle caps
In a tarpaper shack under the cold trees
Of my grave.

I still feel half drunk,
And all those old women beyond my window
Are hunching toward the graveyard.

Drunk, mumbling Hungarian,
The sun staggers in,
And his big stupid face pitches
Into the stove.
For two hours I have been dreaming

Of green butterflies searching for diamonds
In coal seams;
And children chasing each other for a game
Through the hills of fresh graves.
But the sun has come home drunk from the sea,
And a sparrow outside
Sings of the Hanna Coal Co. and the dead moon.
The filaments of cold light bulbs tremble
In music like delicate birds.
Ah, turn it off.

Number Two: i try to waken and greet the world once again

In a pine tree,
A few yards away from my window sill,
A brilliant blue jay is springing up and down, up and down,
On a branch.
I laugh, as I see him abandon himself
To entire delight, for he knows as well as I do
That the branch will not break.

LYING IN A HAMMOCK AT WILLIAM DUFFY'S FARM IN PINE ISLAND, MINNESOTA

Over my head, I see the bronze butterfly,
Asleep on the black trunk,
Blowing like a leaf in green shadow.
Down the ravine behind the empty house,
The cowbells follow one another
Into the distances of the afternoon.
To my right,
In a field of sunlight between two pines,
The droppings of last year's horses
Blaze up into golden stones.
I lean back, as the evening darkens and comes on.

A chicken hawk floats over, looking for home.
I have wasted my life.

TO THE POETS IN NEW YORK

You stroll in the open, leisurely and alone,
Daydreaming of a beautiful human body
That had undressed quietly and slipped into the river
And become the river.
The proud body of an animal that would transform
The snaggled gears and the pulleys
Into a plant that grows under water.
You go searching gently for the father of your own agony,
The camelia of your death.

You keep a dark counsel.
It is not seemly a man should rend open by day
The huge roots of his blood trees.
A man ought to hide sometimes on the banks
Of the sky,
And some human beings
Have need of lingering back in the fastidious half light
Even at dawn.

Solitary,
Patient for the last voices of the dusk to die down, and the dusk
To die down,
Listeners waiting for courteous rivers
To rise and be known.

Notes on the Poets

A. R. AMMONS, born 1926 in Whiteville, North Carolina, went to Wake
Forest College and, later, the University of California. He has taught
school and been in business; currently, he teaches at Cornell. His first
book was *Ommateum* (1955). He then published *Expressions of Sea
Level* (1964), *Corsons Inlet* (1965), and, in that same year, the prob-
lematic and improvisatory poetic journal called *Tape for the Turn of
the Year*. His most recent volume is *Northfield Poems* (1966).

JOHN ASHBERY, born 1927 in Rochester, New York, educated at Har-
vard and Columbia, has lived for most of the last decade in Paris, where
he worked as an art critic. Two years ago, he returned to New York
to edit *Art News;* aside from his poetry and art criticism, he has
written plays in verse and prose. His first book, *Some Trees*, was
published in the Yale Younger Poets Series in 1956. Since then, he
has published *The Tennis Court Oath* (1962) and *Rivers and Moun-
tains* (1966). Ashbery is one of the most profoundly inventive poets
of his time, and his recent work has moved away from the cuts and
ellipses that made some of his poetry as difficult as it is radiant.

GREGORY CORSO, born 1930 in New York City, self-educated, has
lived in various places in this country and in Europe. Among his books
are *The Vestal Lady on Brattle* (1955), *Gasoline* (1958), *The Happy
Birthday of Death* (1960), *Long Live Man* (1962), and a novel,
American Express.

DONALD DAVIE, born 1922 in Yorkshire, England, educated at Cam-
bridge, has taught in Dublin, at Cambridge, on several visits to the
United States and, most recently, at the University of Essex, where he
is professor of literature and dean of comparative studies. He is famed
as a critic as well as a poet: his two best-known studies are *Purity of
Diction in English Verse* and *Articulate Energy*. He has translated
poetry from Slavic languages. His books include *Brides of Reason*
(1955), *A Winter Talent* (1957), *New and Selected Poems* (1961),
and *Events and Wisdoms* (1965).

ROBERT DAWSON, born 1941 in Minnesota, grew up in California and attended Harvard, where he edited *The Harvard Advocate*. He now lives in San Francisco. *Six Mile Corner* was published in 1966, and displayed a hopeful power of poetic organization to bring a sense of self and knowledge of a world into a meaningful relationship.

JAMES DICKEY, born 1923 in Atlanta, Georgia, studied at Vanderbilt University. He has been a college athlete, fighter pilot (in World War II and Korea), advertising executive, sportsman, and, most recently, college teacher at Reed and the University of Wisconsin, among others. He is at present Consultant in Poetry to the Library of Congress. *Into the Stone* (1957) was followed by *Drowning with Others* (1962) and then, in rapid succession, *Helmets* (1964), *Buckdancer's Choice* (1965), and *Poems, 1957–1967*. One of the best poets of the war between civilization and rural nature of his generation, his most recent work exhibits a formal broadening that reflects a movement away from the discursive and toward new sorts of continuity.

ALVIN FEINMAN, born 1929 in New York City, studied philosophy at Yale and taught there briefly before returning to a quiet meditative life in New York. *Preambles and Other Poems*, his only book, was published in 1964. Feinman's poems are perhaps the most difficult of those in this collection. Their difficulty is not that of allusion, nor of ellipsis, nor of problematical form, however, but the phenomenological difficulty of confronting the boundary of the visual and the truly visionary.

ALLEN GINSBERG, born 1926 in Newark, New Jersey, graduated from Columbia College in 1948 and has been a seaman and world traveler. His career as a man of letters and as a living presence is as remarkable as his poetry, which, starting with *Howl* in 1956, astonished poets and audiences with its incantatory modes and its assimilation of Whitman and French symbolist poetry alike to a personal voice. *Kaddish and Other Poems* (1960) followed, together with *Empty Mirror* in the same year and *Reality Sandwiches* (1963), both of which contained some earlier poetry. A volume of his hortatory essays is soon to be published.

ALLEN GROSSMAN, born 1932 in Minneapolis, Minnesota, attended Harvard and edited *The Harvard Advocate*; currently he teaches at Brandeis University. His books are *A Harlot's Hire* (1961) and *The*

Recluse (1965). They reveal not only a massive moral power that never escapes imaginative control, but a notable stylistic growth from an original influence of Robert Lowell.

THOM GUNN, born 1929 in Gravesend, England, attended Cambridge University. For the past 10 years, he has lived in the United States, most recently in Berkeley, California, where he teaches at the University of California. His books are *Fighting Terms* (1954), *The Sense of Movement* (1958), in which he began to show a meditative interest in the violent motion of American life, *My Sad Captains* (1961), and, in 1966, *Positives*. This last is a collaboration with his brother, Ander Gunn, a photographer, in which pictures and text face and explore each other.

ANTHONY HECHT, born 1922 in New York City, studied at Kenyon College and, after his World War II service in Europe, at Columbia. He has lived in Rome, and taught at Smith and Bard Colleges; at present he teaches at the University of Rochester. *A Summoning of Stones* (1954) was followed only after the most exacting and devoted years of work by *The Hard Hours* in 1967. A poet of rich formal elegance in his earlier work, he has developed in his recent poems an intensity that moves beyond his first ironies with no loss of formal control.

DARYL HINE, born 1936 in Burnaby, British Columbia, studied at McGill University and the University of Chicago, where he currently teaches. He has lived in Europe and written both fiction (*The Prince of Darkness and Co.*, published in 1961) and a travel book (*Polish Subtitles*, in 1962). His books of poetry are *Five Poems* (1954), *The Carnal and the Crane* (1957), *The Devil's Picture Book* (1961), and *The Wooden Horse* (1965). His wit, learning, and formal assurance are prodigious, and like Jay MacPherson, his fellow Canadian, evokes a mythological power.

JOHN HOLLANDER, born 1929 in New York City, attended Columbia College, Indiana University, and Harvard, and has taught at Connecticut College, Yale, and Hunter College; he now lives in New York. *A Crackling of Thorns* was published in the Yale Series of Younger Poets in 1958. His other books are *Movie-Going and Other Poems* (1962), *Visions from the Ramble* (1965), and *The Quest of the Gole* (1966). His forthcoming volume is *Types of Shape*.

A. D. HOPE, born 1907 at Cooma, New South Wales, Australia, grew up in Tasmania and studied at the Universities of Sydney and Oxford. After a career of teaching and vocational psychology, he became Professor of English at the Australian National University. His first volume of poetry was *The Wandering Islands,* published in 1955; since then, *Poems* (1960) and *Collected Poems* (1966) have brought him fame, not only as Australia's foremost poet, but as one of the finest writing in English. He is at once a master of iambic verse, at a time when so many have abandoned it, and one of the great poets of heterosexual eroticism of any time.

RICHARD HOWARD, born 1929 in Cleveland, Ohio, attended Columbia College, where he edited *Columbia Review,* has lived in France, and now makes his home in New York City. An outstanding translator of contemporary French literature, he is the author of *Quantities* (1962) and of a forthcoming volume, *The Damages.* He is also at work on a study of recent American poetry and on a collection of dramatic monologues. He is a writer of bewildering energy and Mandarin sparkle.

TED HUGHES, born 1930 in Yorkshire, England, took a B.A. at Cambridge. He spent some time in the United States, published *The Hawk in the Rain* in 1957 and *Lupercal* in 1960. His newest book appeared this year. Its title is *Wodwo.*

KENNETH KOCH, born 1925 in Cincinnati, Ohio, attended Harvard and Columbia Universities, and now teaches at the latter. He has lived in France and Italy, and has a wide knowledge of contemporary French poetry; along with John Ashbery and the late Frank O'Hara, q.q.v., he has shown some of its influences, not only in his associations with painters and his joyful experimentalism, but in his work for the avant-garde theatre as well. His mock-epic, *Ko, or a Season on Earth,* appeared in 1959, *Thank You and Other Poems* in 1962, and *Bertha,* a collection of plays from which the two improvisatory texts here included were taken, in 1966. His comical poems are unmatched.

JAY MacPHERSON, born 1931 in Canada, studied, and now teaches, at Victoria College of the University of Toronto. Her only book of poems, *The Boatman* (1957), is marked not only by wit but by a mythological power with which her short lyrics are resonant.

JAMES MERRILL, born 1926 in New York City, went to Amherst College, served in the U.S. Army and traveled widely before making his home in Stonington, Connecticut, where he now lives. *First Poems* appeared in 1951, *The Country of a Thousand Years of Peace* in 1959, *Water Street* in 1962, and *Nights and Days* in 1966. He has also written novels (*The Seraglio*, published in 1957, and *The [Diblos] Notebook*, in 1965) and plays. Merrill's poetry has grown consistently more intense as his explorations of the psyche have emerged in longer, more ambitious poems of a sustained meditational temper but with great rhetorical variety.

W. S. MERWIN, born 1927 in New York City, grew up in New Jersey and Pennsylvania. He went to Princeton, worked as a tutor in France, Portugal, and Majorca, and has lived much of the last ten years in England and in the south of France. He is a brilliant and copious translator of romance poetry, having published among others *The Poem of the Cid* (1959), *Spanish Ballads* and *The Satires of Persius* (1960), and *The Song of Roland* (1963). His first book, *A Mask for Janus*, won the Yale Younger Poets award for 1952; then followed *The Dancing Bears* (1954), *Green with Beasts* (1956), *The Drunk in the Furnace* (1960), *The Moving Target* (1963), and *The Lice* (1967). His recent poetry has moved further and further away from the full, discursive style of his first four books.

FRANK O'HARA, born 1926 in Baltimore, Maryland, attended Harvard and the University of Michigan after serving in the Navy in World War II. He worked for the Museum of Modern Art in New York, where he was an associate curator of exhibitions at the time of his accidental death in 1966. By then he had published, besides such art criticism as a monograph on Jackson Pollock, *A City Winter and Other Poems* (1952), *Meditations in an Emergency* (1957), *Second Avenue*, a long poem, (1960), *Odes* (1960), and *Lunch Poems* (1965). Like his friends Kenneth Koch and John Ashbery, he worked out of the traditions of French surrealist and later poetry, bringing to his visions of the crises of urban life the holiest kind of playfulness.

SYLVIA PLATH, born 1932 in Boston, educated at Smith and at Newnham College, Cambridge, died in England in 1963. *The Colossus* was first published in England, then in America in 1962. She spent the last years of her life in Devon; the final months of it were devoted to an extraordinary and prolonged burst of imaginative creation which produced the powerful and frequently appalling intensities of the poems in *Ariel* (1966), from which the selection in this anthology has been made.

ADRIENNE RICH, born 1929 in Baltimore, Maryland, attended Radcliffe. Her first book, *A Change of World*, was published in 1951 in the Yale Younger Poets Series; thereafter, *The Diamond Cutters* (1955) and *Snapshots of a Daughter-in-Law* (1963) extended her reputation for precision, humor, and clarity. She has lived in Cambridge, Mass., Holland, and now in New York, and teaches at Swarthmore College. She has translated contemporary Dutch poetry and, in *Necessities of Life* (1966), demonstrated a formal and rhetorical compactness in the service of a growing wisdom.

FREDERICK SEIDEL, born 1936 in St. Louis, Missouri, attended Harvard and edited *The Harvard Advocate*, lived abroad and was associated with *The Paris Review*, and now makes his home in New York City. *Final Solutions* was published in 1963; its dramatic monologues are both topical and apocalyptic.

DAVID SHAPIRO, born 1947 in Newark, New Jersey, still attends Columbia College, where he studied literature and music and continues to expand his capabilities as a concert violinist. *January* (1965) showed both an engaging precocity and a sophisticated ability to use the influences of older poets such as Kenneth Koch and John Ashbery in the interests of his own voice.

JON SILKIN, born 1930 in London, went to the University of Leeds and has since lectured there and at Newcastle-upon-Tyne. He has spent time in the United States, and founded and co-edited the literary quarterly *Stand*. He has published *The Peaceable Kingdom* (1954), *The Two Freedoms* (1958), *The Re-Ordering of the Stones* (1961), *Nature with Man* (1965), and *Poems, New and Selected* in 1966. The *Flower Poems* included in this most recent collection mark a modulation of the relentless questioning and occasional exultant bitterness in his earlier work.

LOUIS SIMPSON, born 1923 in Jamaica, B.W.I., was educated at Columbia, fought in the infantry in France in World War II, returned to Columbia where he edited *Columbia Review*, and published *The Arrivistes* by himself in Paris. He subsequently worked in publishing, then went to California, where he taught at Berkeley for some years, and has just returned to the east to teach at the University of New York at Stony Brook. The lyrical charm and wryness of his war poems gave way to a growing concern with the problematic relation of America's landscape to its civilization. He has published a novel, *Riverside Drive* (1962), and the following books of poetry: *Good News of Death* (1955), *A Dream of Governors* (1959), and *At the End of the Open Road* (1963).

W. D. SNODGRASS, born 1926 in Wilkinsburg, Pennsylvania, studied at Geneva College and the State University of Iowa. He has taught at Cornell, the University of Rochester, and, currently, at Wayne State University in Detroit. *Heart's Needle*, which appeared in 1959, struck critics with its ease, grace, and a tactful honesty that allowed autobiographical material to become lyric poetry without intervening posturing. Albeit in a personal way, he seemed to represent in American poetry some of the qualities that had made Philip Larkin so important in England. Since then, his tone and imaginative concerns have deepened. A new volume is to be published this year.

GARY SNYDER, born 1930 in San Francisco, California, studied at Reed College and at the University of California. He continued his training in Oriental languages for many years in Japan. His poetry is full of the presence of the American Northwest, its landscape, its aboriginal inhabitants, and the Asia that lies, somehow, to the west of it. His books include *Riprap* (1959), *Myths and Texts* (1960), and *A Range of Poems* (1967).

MARK STRAND, born 1934 in Prince Edward Island, Canada, attended Antioch College and studied painting at Yale. From 1959 on, he has devoted himself to poetry, writing, and teaching at the State University of Iowa and Mount Holyoke College among others, and spending a year in Brazil. *Sleeping with One Eye Open* was published in 1964.

MAY SWENSON, born 1919 in Logan, Utah, graduated from Utah State University and has lived since then in New York City. She has worked in publishing, and written fiction and drama as well as verse. Her books are: *Another Animal* (1954), *A Cage of Spines* (1958), *To Mix with Time* (1963), and *Half Sun Half Sleep* (1967), as well as *Poems to Solve*, for children, in 1966. Her work shows a continuing concern both for emblems and signatures in nature and for an ingenious proliferation of poetic shapes and formats.

CHARLES TOMLINSON, born 1927 in Stoke-on-Trent, England, took a degree at Cambridge, taught elementary school in London, lived for a while in Italy, visited the U.S., and now lectures at the University of Bristol. His work reflects a great interest in twentieth-century American poetry, and it is significant that his second volume, *Seeing Is Believing,* was published originally in the United States in 1958. Other books are *The Necklace* (1955), *A Peopled Landscape* (1963), and the forthcoming *American Scenes.*

CHRIS WALLACE-CRABBE, born 1934 in Melbourne, Australia, studied at the University of Melbourne, where he now teaches. Well known as a critic of contemporary Australian literature as well as a poet, he spent 1965–1966 in the United States. *The Music of Division* was published in 1959 and *In Light and Darkness* in 1964.

JAMES WRIGHT, born 1927 in Martin's Ferry, Ohio, went to Kenyon College and the University of Washington, has lived in Austria, and taught at the University of Minnesota. Currently he lives in New York City and is a member of the English Department of Hunter College. *The Green Wall* was published in the Yale Series of Younger Poets in 1957 and was followed by *Saint Judas* in 1959 and *The Branch Will Not Break* (1963). He has translated from German and Spanish prose and poetry, and his own poems have, in recent years, developed amazing but unobtrusive formal resources for the handling of images.